LINCOLNSHIR

Walter Marsden

LINCOLNSHIRE

B. T. Batsford
London

First published 1977

Photoset by
Weatherby Woolnough, Wellingborough, Northants
Printed by
J. W. Arrowsmith Ltd., Bristol
for the publishers B. T. Batsford Ltd
4 Fitzhardinge Street, London W1H 0AH
ISBN 0 7134 0683 6

Contents

Acknowledgments

My warm thanks go to those who helped with information for this book. So many of them went out of their way to provide interesting material or indicate where it could be found. Alphabetically, they include: F. T. Baker, O.B.E., formerly Director, City of Lincoln Libraries, Museum and Art Gallery; The Superintendent, Belton House, Grantham; The Borough Librarian, Boston; Eric Bowser, Holbeach; L. I. Clark, Boston; County Planning Officer of the former Lindsey County Council, Lincoln; Richard Elliott, National Coal Board Geologist, Eastwood; Laurence Elvin, Keeper of the Local Collection, City of Lincoln Libraries, Museum and Art Gallery; James S. English, Librarian, Gainsborough; G. H. Evans, Warden, Gibraltar Point; The Agent, Grimsthorpe Estate, Bourne; W. E. R. Hallgarth, Scartho, Grimsby; Robert Hart, Ministry of Agriculture, Fisheries and Food, Kirton; Mr and Mrs W. H. Hosford, Sleaford; Mr and Mrs D. W. Houlston, Eagle; Richard Janion, Louth; Malcolm G. Knapp, Grantham; The Lincolnshire River Authority, Boston; A. W. Mardon, Ministry of Agriculture, Fisheries and Food, Lincoln; Hugh D. Martineau, Woodhall Spa; Miss F. A. Murray, O.B.E., formerly of the Lindsey and Holland Rural Community Council, Lincoln; National Farmers' Union, Woodhall Spa; David N. Robinson, Louth; P. G. Robinson, Sleaford; A. E. Smith, O.B.E., for so long prominent in nature conservation in Lincolnshire, and beyond; Michael Thompson, Holbeach Hurn.

Acknowledgments

Besides consulting standard works on Lincolnshire, I have learned much from the files of *Lincolnshire Life,* a wide range of brochures, notably the publications of the Lincolnshire Industrial Archaeology Group, the "Nature Reserves Handbook" of the Lincolnshire Trust for Nature Conservation Ltd, and historians of Lincoln, Boston, Louth, Gainsborough, Sleaford, Stamford, Tetney and Eagle, as well as leaflets prepared for various parish churches.

Thanks are also due to the following for permission to reproduce the illustrations in the book: Peter Baker Photography, nos 3, 20, 23; J. Allan Cash Ltd, nos 9, 10, 11, 13, 17, 24; A. F. Kersting, F.R.P.S., nos 2, 5, 7, 14, 15, 16, 18, 19, 21, 22, 25, 26; Barnaby's Picture Library (Mustography), no. 6; Kenneth Scowen, F.I.I.P., F.R.P.S., nos 8, 12; E. W. Tattersall, no. 1; no. 4 is from the publishers' files. The map is by Patrick Leeson.

Illustrations

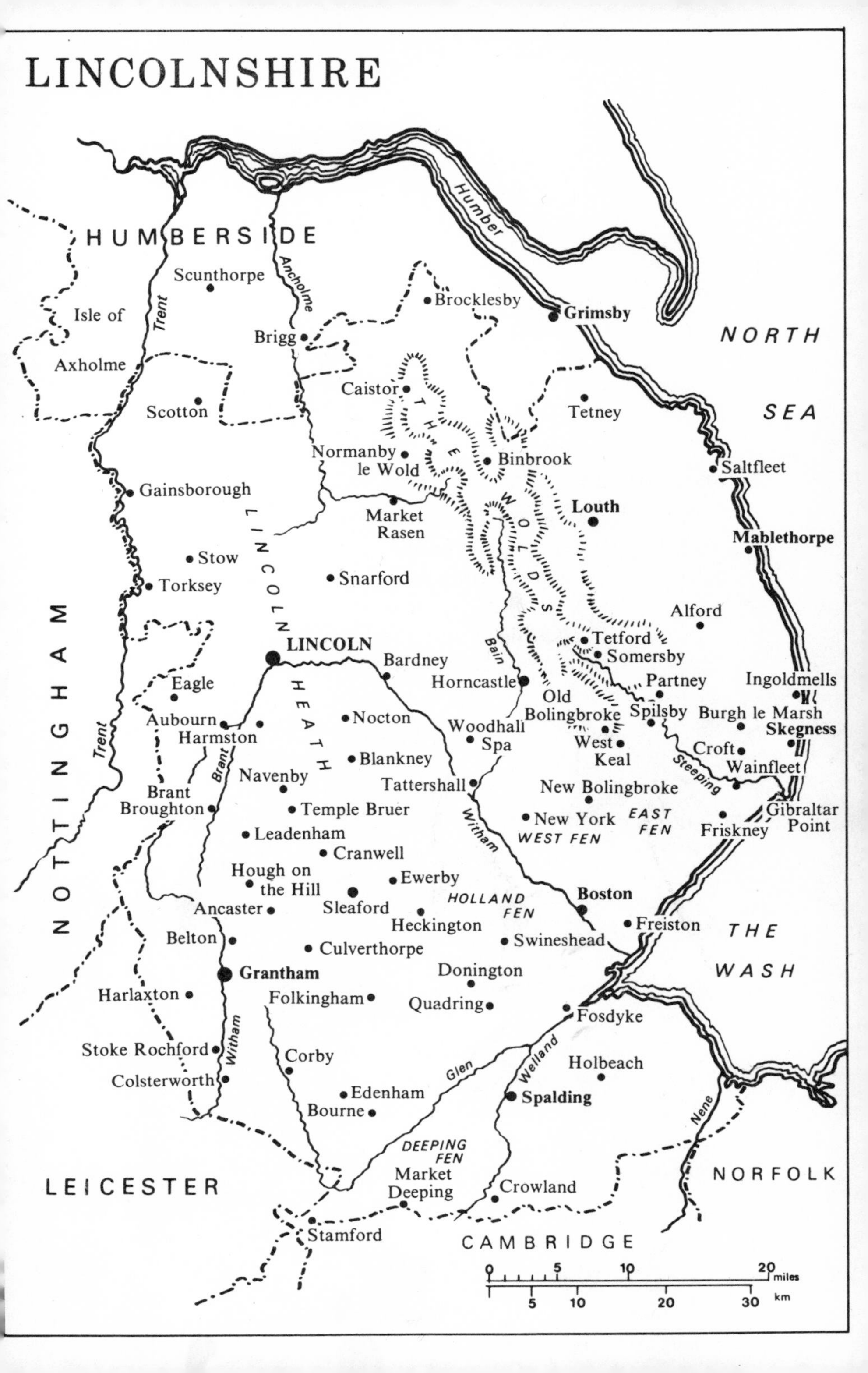
LINCOLNSHIRE
HUMBERSIDE
Humber
Scunthorpe
Ancholme
Brocklesby
Grimsby
Isle of
Axholme
Trent
Brigg
NORTH
SEA
Caistor
Scotton
Tetney
THE WOLDS
Normanby
le Wold
Binbrook
Saltfleet
Gainsborough
Louth
Market
Rasen
Mablethorpe
LINCOLN HEATH
Stow
Torksey
Snarford
Alford
NOTTINGHAM
Bain
Tetford
Somersby
LINCOLN
Bardney
Horncastle
Partney
Ingoldmells
Eagle
Old
Bolingbroke
Spilsby
Burgh le Marsh
Skegness
Aubourn
Harmston
Nocton
Woodhall
Spa
West
Keal
Croft
Steeping
Wainfleet
Blankney
Brant
Navenby
Tattershall
New Bolingbroke
Brant
Broughton
Temple Bruer
Witham
New York
EAST
FEN
Gibraltar
Point
Friskney
WEST FEN
Leadenham
Cranwell
Hough on
the Hill
Ewerby
Sleaford
HOLLAND
FEN
Boston
Ancaster
Heckington
Freiston
THE
WASH
Belton
Swineshead
Culverthorpe
Grantham
Donington
Harlaxton
Folkingham
Quadring
Fosdyke
Welland
Witham
Stoke Rochford
Holbeach
Corby
Glen
Colsterworth
Edenham
Spalding
Bourne
Nene
DEEPING
FEN
Market
Deeping
NORFOLK
LEICESTER
Crowland
Stamford
CAMBRIDGE
0
5
10
20
miles
5
10
20
30
km

For my Lincolnshire friends,
especially
Betty Coy
Clare Fleming
Kathleen and Philip Gipps
Neil Wright

Introduction

Suppose that somewhere in England you see a stretch of heather, bracken and wavy hair grass, with mosses and lichens in patches which have been grazed bare. Ahead of you, tufts of cotton grass and spiky sedges grow in a marshy area. From such details you could be forgiven for assuming that this is a Pennine or some other northern moor. But it cannot be, for one thing because the soil is sandy. In fact it is a tract of Lincolnshire heathland near Woodhall Spa.

Or again, your car has climbed a couple of hundred feet up a very steep hill, and at the top, but still below the larks, you sit on the short grass among the chalk plants. Down in the valley are farm-houses and fields, a small river, a fine country mansion or two, a few groupings scarcely important enough to be called hamlets. The chalk scarp and the valley, the turf and the plants suggest Box Hill above the river Mole in Surrey. However, if you look at the chalk in a nearby disused quarry, you see under the top white layer an unusual seam of chalk which is red. You are on Red Hill, opposite Stenigot's radar dishes, on the western edge of the Lincolnshire Wolds.

To identify the location of a third area would be even more difficult from a brief description. You are in an oak wood, though in places ash and wych elm challenge for supremacy. Coppices of hazel hold dog-rose, guelder rose and honeysuckle. Much of the ground is damp, rich in ferns, mosses and flowers. The rides too have their special plant life. The area could be almost anywhere that a remnant of old deciduous woodland survives on a clay soil, though the traditional mixture of coppice with standards of oak and ash being restored here is now all too uncommon. It is Hoplands Wood at Claxby by Alford, below the eastern edge of the Wolds.

These three examples have been chosen almost at random to illustrate the variety of landscape in Lincolnshire. Lincolnshire is far from being 'all flats, fogs and fens', in the phrase of George III. Not that there is anything wrong with flat country, as any Dane or Dutchman will testify. Flat country need not be dismissed as dreary or boring. Great numbers of holidaymakers enjoy the level miles of sand on the Lincolnshire coast, and the strange beauty of the Lincolnshire Fens is becoming appreciated now that thousands of visitors go there to see the spring bulb fields.

It might be objected that the three areas singled out are exceptions. So in a sense they are; they are what large tracts of Lincolnshire and other parts of England used to be like. We should not have such a clear picture of the past and could not understand the processes which have modified it if these and companion areas had been lost. These particular sites happen to be nature reserves managed by the Lincolnshire Trust for Nature Conservation, which is the third oldest in the country. Much information about wildlife and its conservation is available to members.

The Trust has a charming symbol of two lapwings in flight. To Lincolnshire folk the lapwings are not known affectionately as peewits; to our ears their call is pye-wipe. That thin, forlorn cry as our pyewipes loop and tumble above the pastures, the acres of peas, potatoes, sugar beet, corn, poultry or tulips, is a lament that Lincolnshire is not what it was.

For about a thousand years until 1974 Lincolnshire had been a rectangle in eastern England measuring some 75 miles from north to south by up to 45 miles from west to east. It was so big that, like Yorkshire, it was divided into three units, known as the Parts of Lindsey, of Kesteven and of Holland. There was a natural boundary on the north, the Humber estuary, and on the east was the North Sea, from the Humber down to about half-way round the Wash. To the west the Trent and, to the south, the Fenland rivers Welland and Nene, indicated rather than accurately defined Lincolnshire's boundaries. Within these limits in 1971 there were 808,384 people living on 1,704,529 acres.

In 1974 local government reorganisation meant that Lincolnshire lost to Humberside a strip of territory south of the estuary; a quarter of a million acres had to be given up, with 300,000 people and £16¼ million in rateable value (leaving the county in its new form with only about £17½ million). The main industrial region was lost. Grimsby has gone, formerly our largest town and for long the world's premier fishing port; and Scunthorpe, the largest iron and steel project in Europe; and Immingham, the most rapidly developing port, the biggest coal-handling terminal, busy too with ore and chemicals. We have lost the birthplace of one of Lincolnshire's very greatest sons—John Wesley—at Epworth, with the surrounding district of the Isle of Axholme, not to mention the market towns of Brigg and Kirton in Lindsey. Other sacrifices include historical associations and architectural treasures.

The government case for Humberside was based largely on expectations of increased industrial development. A new east-west road route was accordingly planned and it was decided in 1969 that a bridge should at last span the Humber. Nevertheless, a poll of electors in North Lincolnshire showed that only just over a quarter of them were in favour of joining the new county of Humberside. They seemed to agree with Lindsey County Council that 'Patterns of development and travel, and considerations of common interest through links of employment, shopping and social activities and through history and tradition, all point to an affinity between each bank of the Humber and its hinterland but to a total lack of real affinity between the opposite sides of the estuary'.

Despite all the arguments against it, however, the Local Government Bill was passed, and Lincolnshire's boundaries were amended. With much regret, I have decided not to deal with the many interesting places now lost but still widely regarded as belonging to Lincolnshire. Whatever the past, they now lie outside the county. It seems sensible to deal with Lincolnshire as it is.

To do so, I have quartered the county by car and on foot, reviving memories and gaining new impressions; with these I have combined the observations of others, including many friends. Inevitably many features have had to be passed over. Inevitably less than justice is done to some places, maybe less prettily sited than others, or perhaps lacking outstanding architecture, but in the most workaday places I bore in mind the story about a mother dunlin. The most common of the smaller shore-birds, the dunlin is rather dumpy, black in summer underneath, its back rusty. A dunlin mother was asked to show her chicks, which prompted the exclamation, 'But how ugly they are!' The mother replied in her grating voice, 'To me, they are beautiful'. Much of Lincolnshire is still too little known, so it may be helpful to list the natural divisions and sketch the historical background.

Lowland and upland alternate across most of the county from west to east. The lowlands bordering our shore of the Trent are marked off sharply by a limestone scarp rising about 100 feet. It is popularly known as the Cliff or the Edge. Here, east of the Trent, the limestone is a ridge only a mile or so wide. At Lincoln, which was built on it, there is a big gap through which the river Witham makes a horseshoe curve. A dozen miles south of Lincoln the limestone ridge broadens and becomes known as the Heath. At Ancaster there is another gap; then the uplands rise and spread towards Grantham and Stamford in the south-west of the county. The limestone region may be pictured in outline as a guitar, its body the Heath and its neck, unfortunately much awry, the Cliff. Like other strata in Lincolnshire, the limestone dips eastwards under the neighbouring formation, so there is no steep drop to the next lowland, the valley of the Ancholme (pronounced AN-kum).

East again, another scarp rears up, this time of chalk, the edge of the Lincolnshire Wolds. They are a southerly continuation of the Yorkshire Wolds and part of the chalk uplands slanting across England to Dorset. Officially declared an Area of Outstanding Natural Beauty, the Wolds have had their chalk somewhat covered over by glacial drift material—unlike the South Downs, with which they are sometimes compared. The Wolds in turn drop more gradually to the east, giving way to a coastal plain. The sea has retreated along most of this lowland, leaving a belt inclined to be salty, famous as excellent pasture and known as the Marsh.

The zones thus far considered extend roughly north and south, except for the broad limestone plateau in the south-west. Another exception is found in the south-east: the sea-influenced Marsh spreads out in its southern reach and merges into the Fens, once swamps formed by rivers, and hence not salt. The Fens extend inland from the Wash as far as the chalk Wolds, sweeping round the southern edge of the high ground to link up with the low-lying valley of the river Witham which continues the Ancholme valley. Some fenland was included in the Parts of Kesteven, the bulk of which, however, comprised the limestone plateau. Most of the Fens were within the Parts of Holland. The northern half of the county (a generous half) made up the Parts of Lindsey.

Ice sheets originating in Scandinavia—as we can tell from boulders they carried—ground their way across Lincolnshire, scooping out valleys and then depositing boulder clay in them and also on the marshland and the plateaux. Icebergs floating in what became the Wash are thought to have dumped boulders and rock fragments.

In the long warm period after the second of the four Ice Ages generally recognised, primitive man appeared in Lincolnshire. Evidence is scanty until Mesolithic times, perhaps 10,000 years ago, when we know certainly of settlement in Lincolnshire. For instance, Mesolithic hunters and fishers who used small flint implements, found themselves a sandy locality near West Keal, as far south as the Wolds go.

The first farmers, Neolithic stockmen, may have come to Lincolnshire about 2,000 BC. They arrived from the south, the first people to develop the prehistoric trackways, such as the one which followed the Jurassic chalk scarps across England diagonally from the south-west and was given the name of the Jurassic Way. In Lincolnshire another ancient road came from the Fens by Bourne and Sleaford to Lincoln; it is Mareham Lane, still in use as a motor road. We also have Sewstern Lane, from the river Welland to the Trent at Newark; the Salters Way inland from the coast, and tracks along the Wolds, such as Barton Street and High Street. In the Wolds too are barrows: long barrows and the later round barrows of the Beaker Folk.

These pugnacious Bronze Age intruders came at the end of a wet period. Later bronze users enjoying a drier climate were able to settle more of the valleys and even the Fens. Successors to the Beaker Folk were skilful smiths, judging by such finds as the bronze shield from the Witham near Lincoln and by founders' hoards at Caythorpe and elsewhere. We know of Iron Age farming on the Marsh and in the Fens, of saltings on the coast and of an important nucleus at Sleaford, with a mint, as well as one hilltop fort definitely of this period, at Honington covering the Ancaster Gap. For the first time we know, or think we know, the name of the people inhabiting most of Lincolnshire. They werewere, we think, the Coritani. They were conquered by the Romans without difficulty before AD 50.

As they came, the Romans pushed their roads across the country, following the already ancient routes more faithfully than is always recognised but not necessarily using the tracks. The Roman Fosse Way from Exeter and Cirencester joined the Ermine Street from London at Lincoln, and Ermine Street was continued to the Humber. That was, of course, after the Romans had taken over the Iron Age settlement at Lincoln, on the noble site where the cathedral now stands, and had embellished and extended it for 300 years. Also at Lincoln they made a drainage channel, the Sincil Dyke, in an effort (not entirely successful) to control flooding by the Witham. A more ambitious project was the canal, the Fosse Dyke, they cut from the Witham to the Trent, still busy despite vicissitudes. Then too the Romans began to drain the Fens for cornland, and constructed a great channel nearly sixty miles long, the Carr Dyke, from the Fens to the Witham near Lincoln. At Stamford, Ancaster and Caistor they had camps. In time they built many villas, choosing the kind of site which appealed hundreds of years later to the gentry for their country houses. Iron deposits the Romans worked are still being exploited, and the stone they quarried at Ancaster has been in demand for building ever since.

Towards the end of the Roman period some places in Lincolnshire, among them Caistor and Horncastle, were given defensive walls. It was too late. The legions left, the association with Rome and Christianity was broken and a northern pagan influence was established. Lincolnshire did not suffer from the change as much as some other parts of England. Unlike the Romans, who came to

1 & 2. Lincolnshire north and south: the Wolds near Binbrook and tulip fields near Spalding

conquer, the tribes of Friesians, Saxons and especially Angles came to settle and to farm. They left the towns to decay and populated the countryside. It was their bad luck that the climate became wetter, drowning parts of the Fens, but they established villages in many districts, particularly along the edge of the limestone. One grouping set up the kingdom of Lindsey, north of Lincoln. At times the Mercians overran it, at other times the Northumbrians, but somehow it survived for a couple of hundred years. The kingdom had a bishop from AD 678, some 50 years after mass baptisms in the Trent by Paulinus, the delegate of St Augustine. Monasteries were founded at such places as Crowland and Bardney. In the 9th century they were destroyed by the Danes.

Before AD 800 the Danes had begun to raid England, using the Humber and the Wash for their main thrusts. The bishopric of Lindsey ended for a time, the bishop of Leicester taking over; but he withdrew far to the south, to Dorchester on Thames. The raids grew in intensity and changed to invasion and occupation. Eventually about half the population of Lincolnshire was Danish. As well as the English villages with names including 'ing' (Spalding, Corringham, Billingborough), there were upwards of 250 villages with the Danish ending '-by' and many others with 'thorpe', meaning a secondary settlement. Lincoln and Stamford were two of the Five Burghs in the Danelaw (the others being Nottingham, Derby and Leicester). The sons and successors of Alfred the Great recovered the Danelaw but there was a second conquest by Canute, son of Svein, who had made Gainsborough his beach-head in 1013. Now Lincolnshire prospered by being linked to the flourishing commerce of Scandinavia.

The link was, as everybody knows, broken in 1066 by the Normans. William the Conqueror had little trouble in Lincolnshire, except in the Fens, where Hereward the Wake organised resistance (at first with Danish support) for a time. At Lincoln, William founded a castle, brought the bishop—now a Norman—back from Dorchester and supported him in founding a cathedral. From the Domesday survey it is clear that Lincolnshire had a large population yet had land to spare for development on the Marsh and in the Fens; a high proportion of free peasants, and flourishing towns, notably Lincoln and Stamford. Lincolnshire was wealthy. The Normans

3. Louth church, considered to have 'the finest spire in England'

fastened greedily on the county, holding it down from the castles they built, among them Bolingbroke, Spalding and Folkingham. During Norman times many monasteries were established. The population continued to grow; the area under cultivation increased, in large part through reclamation. The Fens and the Wolds came to support large numbers of sheep, for although much corn was grown, the chief emphasis was on the production of wool. Thanks to wool, the towns thrived as well as the countryside. Great fairs were held at Boston, Stamford and Lincoln, attracting foreign merchants from Norway, Flanders, Germany, Italy and Spain.

The fourteenth century saw changes for the worse: the Black Death of 1369, the Hundred Years War against France, and most of all a shift of trade from Scandinavia, for which Lincolnshire ports were well placed, to more southerly European markets. The cumulative effect of such developments affected Lincolnshire towns badly, especially Lincoln itself.

Difficulties continued until the eighteenth century. It is sufficient perhaps to mention the Wars of the Roses, when Stamford and Grantham were sacked, and the troubles associated with the dissolution of the religious houses, marked by disorders in 1536 at Louth, Horncastle, Boston, Sleaford and Lincoln. In the Civil War, Lincolnshire's strategic position, between the Parliamentarian stronghold of East Anglia and Royalist centres in the midlands and north involved many skirmishes, some of them serious, as at Winceby, while Lincoln changed hands more than once.

Two other setbacks took place during this long period. They concerned the Fens and, to a lesser extent, the Marsh. In the fifteenth century and again during the Civil War, there was troublesome flooding. The earlier disaster had natural causes, the later was man-made. Ever since Roman times at least, attempts to reclaim the swamps had been going on. Most of them were undertaken by villagers working together, making banks to keep out the water and ditches to ease its flow and keeping channels clear. Large-scale drainage by landowners in the Ancholme valley and the Parts of Holland was undertaken at the end of Elizabeth I's reign, under James I and Charles I. Charles also devised a plan to raise money uncontrolled by Parliament through reclaiming the Fens. He obtained funds from numbers of 'Participants' to whom he granted in return large tracts of land they were to drain. The enterprise was more successful than previous attempts but extremely unpopular with the fenmen, who saw in it a threat to their common rights, their fowling, fishing, reed-cutting and, in short, to their old, independent way of life. They seized their opportunity during the Civil War to frustrate the Participant scheme. Without constant maintenance the newly drained land reverted to fen.

Prospects for Lincolnshire's future were disheartening, and change for the better came slowly, but it came. A combination of factors in the eighteenth century brought new heights of prosperity for about 150 years.

Through the techniques of the so-called Agricultural Revolution, Lincolnshire was enabled to use the land more intensively and to increase production. The Marsh and other famous Lincolnshire pastures, where cattle were fattened for the London market, were supplemented by new grazing areas won by drainage of the Fens, this time aided by pumps worked by windmills, or gained by enclosures. With these enclosures and their miles of hedges, with extended cultivation and drainage, improvements to country estates by parks, ornamental lakes and plantations of trees, the whole landscape was changed, becoming what our own fathers regarded as the typical English scene.

Lincolnshire's increased production helped to meet the demand from the new industrial regions of the Midlands and the North. In turn, Lincolnshire needed supplies of fertilisers and other materials which were not available locally. About the same time there were improvements in transport, first by water and then by land. We have seen that the uplands and valleys of Lincolnshire run north and south; the old roads took the easy way, following the lie of the land, and consequently there were few east-west routes. The turnpike roads altered this by linking up with other roads, encouraging the building of bridges and generally opening up communications from east to west.

These tendencies are interestingly examined by Alan Rogers in his *History of Lincolnshire.* He points out that with the spread of the turnpike network, for the first time Lincolnshire's trade was not dominated by the London markets, which required access to the sea. When the railway came, about the middle of the nineteenth century, Lincolnshire was even more closely connected with the midland and northern industrial centres. In time the railways also opened up the Lincolnshire coast to holiday-makers from these areas.

Steam power brought other far-reaching changes. Applied to Fenland pumps, steam ensured for the first time something like adequate control of flooding. Applied to agriculture, steam speeded, extended and increased production. Thanks also to steam, new industries were set up in the major towns, such as the railway workshops at Grantham and the manufacture of agricultural machinery there, at Lincoln, Gainsborough and Stamford.

However, the drift from the land was going on, and the depopulation of villages reached new proportions. Imports of cheap foreign corn, combined with other developments, caused an agri-cutural depression which lasted for several generations. There were industrial crises, bankruptcies and unemployment.

In our times, certain changes are obvious, even if their long-term results are not. Agriculture has prospered again, especially arable farming. More intensive mechanisation, demanding high capital outlay, has led to the creation of very large farms with fields which have been described as 'hedgeless and treeless arable prairies'. On the other hand, in the Fens, smallholdings have survived, thanks in part to the remarkable expansion of bulb-growing and similar projects. Agriculture remains Lincolnshire's mainstay, more so than ever now that Humberside has most of the other industries which had been built up. How Lincolnshire will fare is debated by pessimists and optimists (of whom I am one). Our subject here, though, is present-day Lincolnshire and how it came to be as we find it.

ONE

The North Sea Coast and The Marsh

The Coast

Blue sky, blue sea, golden sands: holiday weather as it should be, and on the Lincolnshire coast the chances are that it will be, for we are on the drier side of England. A belt of shore stretching about 20 miles north of Skegness is the part of the county known to more people than any other, for here are some of the finest sandy holiday beaches in Britain. They have attracted holiday-makers and excursionists, especially from the Midlands, for more than a century. Perhaps they are not for those who only want to lie and bake in the sun, because the air is fresh and on the move. As it happens, the visitors tend to come in families, and children too keep on the move.

The holiday-makers tend to stay by the shore, enjoying the sands, promenades, deck chairs, bathing and sunbathing and the facilities provided. As a boy, the poet Tennyson spent family holidays at Mablethorpe, dreaming romantically of the Greek ships beached for the siege of Troy. Later he lost interest in the scene and could 'only find/The drain-cut level of the marshy lea,/Grey sandbanks, and pale sunsets, dreary wind,/Dim shores, dense rains, and heavy-clouded sea'. Yet the shore has a charm of its own. On a fine calm day when the tide is out, the sand is far from being grey, or even uniformly brown, but is dyed with the hues of a crab's shell, a dab's back, of amber and umber. The expanse of sand ends with a low kerb of waves rooting about at its edge like haddock guzzling herring spawn. Beyond is a smooth pavement of water, pale as a jellyfish. Sea and sky merge in a luminous shimmer, where ships hang apparently high above your head.

For all the thousands of people at the beach, the countryside a few miles away is hardly busier than at other seasons. A laudable attempt to interest visitors in what is going on around them has been made by the National Farmers' Union, who co-operate with Butlin's in providing question-and-answer sessions on farming and horticulture in Britain's largest arable county, and in taking parties to see some of the husbandry which is rightly the pride of Lincolnshire.

As a matter of fact there is plenty of interest on the coast itself. Few visitors fail to notice the miles of concrete seawall and the groynes which have been put up to control the devastating effects of a high tide on the coast of Lincolnshire such as occurred in 1571—the subject of Jean Ingelow's famous poem—in 1953 and, to a lesser extent, in 1975. Lives have been lost, houses and other buildings damaged and much other destruction caused. Sutton on Sea was the worst-affected town in 1953, when four and a half feet of mud choked the streets. Since then the sea defences have been strengthened to reinforce the sand dunes and sea banks which line a shore rarely more than 20 feet above sea level all the way northwards from the Wash towards the Humber, and in places no more than a yard or so.

On the whole the currents of the moody North Sea sweep counter-clockwise and some of them pour south past Lincolnshire. Along the holiday portion of the coast the tussle of the waves has been eroding the land for centuries. A church at Skegness was washed away before Tudor times, for instance; Mablethorpe lost its church of St Peter a little later, and Ingoldmells too has suffered encroachment. Altogether thousands of acres of land and five parish churches built in the Middle Ages have gone since the thirteenth century. Striking evidence of the battle with the sea is visible at Trusthorpe, Sutton and several other places when the neap tides are exceptionally low. Then the exposed sand flats are spiky with the stumps and roots of a forest overwhelmed by the sea more than 4,000 years ago. Where the waves break, some of these remains emerge like the necks of a herd of dinosaurs; on the beach they stand, scoured, polished and blackened by sea and sand and time, anachronistically suggesting the ruins of a gigantic trap for invading armies with tanks.

Despite (critics might say) the caravans, the holiday camp and the flying club, Ingoldmells repays a more than casual glance. When the concrete sea defences were being erected, a Roman settlement was unearthed. A palm tree grows near the porch of the medieval church, which has an unusual font, outstanding woodwork and a quaint little brass from 1520 of the cripple William Palmer and his 'stylt', as the inscription calls his crutch. Ingoldmells is also one of the many spots along the Lincolnshire coast where salt was produced from the Iron Age until medieval times and even later. Sea water was boiled in clay pots produced locally—the circular sites remain and have been mistaken for salt pans, which were more often rectangular, as they still are in Mediterranean countries. Salt was of course important for preserving meat in the centuries before fresh meat was available all year round.

It was perhaps even more important for preserving fish, especially herrings. In eastern England we have, as well as the harvest moon and the hunters' moon, the autumn herring moon. By October the herring shoals are spawning off the Lincolnshire coast and their courtship behaviour is stimulated around full moon, when increasing numbers of fish swim up into the light and thus into the drifters' nets.

By then the chalets and caravans are closed after the short holiday season. During their stay the visitors cause serious damage to the dunes which line the coast. The damage is accentuated by the number of people coming for a picnic on day trips by car and coach—two million trips in 1969, and many more by now. It has been calculated by Lindsey County Council that forty people (ten to fifteen car loads) each summer day will wear the vegetation off a dune and expose the sand. Once this has happened, the wind sets to work. Sand is blown away, hissing as it goes, and the erosion is intensified by the speedy formation of a blow-out or hole. The wind-eddies gouge out a funnel, which spreads, undermining the sides of the dune, causing sandslides and thus extending the erosion.

A number of measures are enforced to allow access while preventing or limiting damage. Among them are restrictions on parking, requests to keep to specially sited footpaths, some of them made of railway sleepers, and a number of other sensible rules to protect the ecological, scientific and visual features. In this way it is hoped to retain the present attractive qualities of the coast.

From the golf course south of Skegness a narrow road continues to the Gibraltar Point Nature Reserve. In 1952 15,000 people visited Gibraltar Point; in 1968 180,000 and in 1974 250,000. About fifty years ago the area seemed likely to be drastically altered. A scheme was then afoot for motor racing along the sands from Skegness to Boston. The scheme fell through, but a further threat loomed up: the development of the Tennyson Glen estate at Gibraltar Point. In 1932, however, Lindsey County Council made the far-sighted decision to buy much of the land under the Sandhills Act, the first of its kind in this country, so as to retain it as an open space. In 1949 the Council agreed to a proposal by the newly formed Lincoln shire Trust for Nature Conservation to establish a nature reserve, later extended by the Council and then by the Skegness Urban District Council to comprise 1,500 acres, the first statutory local authority reserve in England. Access is open, subject to bye-laws. For most of the Lincolnshire Trust reserves a member's permit is necessary.

Gibraltar Point is rightly one of the show-places of Lincolnshire. Within the reserve are the most extensive sand dunes in the county. On the older dunes, back from the sea, is the finest expanse of sea buckthorn in the whole country. When I was last there, early in May, my attention was drawn to a rusty looking little bush, a clump of shrubby sea blite which is farther north than any other in Europe. Shore crabs were dodging in and out of the green, spoon-shaped leaves of sea purslane growing on the banks of the creeks. I was also in time for an abundance of Spring Beauty, which used to be called Claytonia, each little white flower on its green stalk which is stuck like a pin through an oval green leaf. It was far too early in the year to see the glory of one of the best sea lavender marshes in Britain, which forms a lovely carpet by the beginning of August. I saw and heard enough skylarks to satisfy Wordsworth, Shelley and Vaughan Williams. I saw whimbrel, and a short-eared owl hunting in day-light. Rare visitors recently included a hoopoe, which remained three days. The sandy beach is one of the last regular nesting places of the Little Tern on the Lincolnshire coast. Terns attract numbers of the pirate seabird, the arctic skua, which harries them into disgorging their food; on a single day in 1972, 65 arctic skuas were seen. Thousands of migratory birds arrive in spring and autumn, following the line of the dunes, settling to rest for a few minutes or a few hours. The autumn flight of pink-footed geese, though diminished, is still spectacular to see and to hear. From the Wash thousands of waders take advantage of the dunes and sand-spits as a high-tide roost to await the ebb. Prominent on the landward side of new dunes are three wire-netting enclosures, the Heligoland bird traps, where nearly 14,000 birds were ringed in 1972; but this was regarded as a disappointing total.

At the Point itself, a promontory, the coast curves to become one shore of the Wash. Just round the corner of the promontory is the mouth of the Steeping River (why not the River Steeping, nobody seems to know), which started out in the Wolds near Somersby as Tennyson's 'brook'—or so some claim—where it is known as the River Lymn. It changes its name after it has left the Wolds and its flow has been canalised. The Steeping River discharges into the sea at Wainfleet Haven.

Across the Wash are the chalk cliffs of Hunstanton, not always visible although the distance is only about twelve miles. On most days much of this distance seems to be taken up by some of the most extensive sand and mud flats in Britain. Common seals are born on the sand shoals and when the tide is out in summer a young seal pup may become stranded on the beach. Don't touch it, for it will doubtless regain the sea at the next high tide. When the tide is in, seals have been known to pop their heads out of the water to watch you as you walk along the shore.

Although so close to Skegness, where the sea erodes the land, Gibraltar Point, like most of the Lincolnshire coast, is literally gaining ground. The sequence can be seen in stages. Sheltered by a spit or ridge of shifting sand off the Point, debris washed up by the sea traps blown sand and very soon plants take hold, from glasswort (locally called samphire) to grasses and so on, helping the formation of a dune. At one place on the beach an anti-tank defence erected in 1940 has already had its iron posts almost completely buried in a dune which developed. These new dunes are extremely vulnerable to erosion. A single family picnicking and playing on a sandhill will cause furrows and slippage.

Behind the new dunes is a salt marsh formed of mud and silt brought by the sea. It is liable to flooding in autumn and winter, sometimes isolating the old coastguard house which is now the Field Station.

The oldest dunes in the reserve are farther from the sea and nearer the road. In 1825, the date of the first one-inch Ordnance Survey map, they were the sea bank, with the beach and sea in front of them. In the shelter of the old sandhill too there was salt marsh. By hard and patient work, salt marsh can be reclaimed and turned into fertile land. An example of this process can be seen at Croft Marsh, inland from the road to Skegness from Gibraltar Point where, since the seventeenth century, good farmland has been won from the marsh.

The Marsh

The area of Lincolnshire known as the Marsh is a strip up to ten miles wide and on average about ten feet above sea level. It is a sort of huge step cut in the chalk by the sea. On it, glaciers have deposited boulder clay and in turn this has a covering of tide-borne silt just back from the coast. Brooks from the Wolds wriggle across the Marsh, sometimes gathering into a larger stream such as the Great Eau. This name is not the French word for water but derives from the Old English 'ea', meaning a stream. As in the Fens, there are dykes, drains and ditches, for in the Marsh too there has been an enormous amount of reclamation over the centuries. Marshland roads are naturally dependent on bridges over the network of waterways and make their way as best they can, with many a right-angle, across the fields from one landmark to another—a church tower or a clump of trees (often occurring together).

In the south the Marsh adjoins the Wolds and the Fens. We can start down there to explore the Marsh.

The pronunciation 'borough', as in Edinburgh, is used for Burgh le Marsh. Despite its title, Burgh has a unique situation in Marshland, as it stands on a hill. From the tower of its church, where eight bells hang, the Wolds can be seen as far as West Keal, and in the other direction, across the Marsh, is the North Sea. Opinions are divided about the brick south porch of the church, some finding it incongruous. There is Jacobean carving on such features as the pulpit and font cover (which has double doors and a gilded bird standing on a book and holding in its beak an object described as an inkhorn or a sandsifter). The lectern was carved in 1874 by Jabez Good, hairdresser, signpainter and author of *A Lincolnshire Glossary.*

Good's book traces the history of the parish, quoting the antiquarian Stukeley's opinion, widely accepted, that Burgh was a Roman castrum guarding the coast against the Saxons. Remains from these periods have been found but the site was inhabited even in Mesolithic times. Many of the prehistoric discoveries were made on Cock Hill, where a cockpit used to be.

It is fitting that Burgh has a local chronicler, for it is a picturesque little town, with a windmill tower on the western approach and at the eastern foot of the hill is a five-sailed mill, bought and restored by the praiseworthy Lindsey County Council. Holiday traffic swirls over the hill in summer, quite disregarding mills and church and the Market Place where the bow-windowed County Library stands among old houses and shops.

One of Jabez Good's comments recalls that 'the General Baptists were numerous in the south marshes of Lincolnshire and they suffered very severely for conscience sake in the reign of Charles II'. Not far from the disused Georgian brick church at Great Steeping in the neighbourhood is the Monksthorpe Baptist Chapel and outdoors baptistry, a pool into which candidates for baptism used to walk. Worship was carried on here after the Disestablishment Act of 1664 had forbidden all religious worship within five miles of an established Church of England. The Burgh Baptists had to close their chapel but Monksthorpe persisted, posting a lookout in a tree to warn of approaching soldiers.

At much the same time a prominent local Baptist, Robert Shalders, was disinterred on the day of his funeral by the inhabitants of Croft, his body dragged on a sledge to be left at his own gate. That is Croft's shame. Croft's glory is its church, by any reckoning one of the major Marsh churches. Like several others, it has much of the original woodwork, here fifteenth century. It also has one of the earliest brasses in the country—perhaps from 1300—showing a mailed knight; and two alabaster monuments to seventeenth-century members of the Browne family, who lived at the Old Hall. The imposing brass eagle lectern was recovered from the moat of the Old Hall some years ago.

The Marsh is indeed a great place for churches, some of them big, despite its lack of building stone. Some of the best known churches are Perpendicular, built in the fourteenth and fifteenth centuries when wealth from wool was available to pay for the carriage of stone by waterways. Not, of course, that all the churches are outwardly imposing; for example, Irby in the Marsh is only sixty feet long, including the tower. In such a small church it is not surprising that the font also is diminutive. It was at Irby that Cox, when researching for his *Little Guide to Lincolnshire* in 1910, 'remarked on its small dimensions to the old dame who was cleaning the church. She replied, "Well, the babies in these parts are mostly small"'.

A bigger church, Bratoft, is by no means easy to find except by trial and error in a tangle of lanes—a pleasant enough task. On the way you can—if you are a member of the Lincolnshire Trust—take in a visit to a small nature reserve known as Heath's Meadows, named after Nurse Heath of Nettleham in recognition of her services in raising funds for the Trust. The interest at Bratoft Ings (the Scandinavian word for meadows) is of course the grassland flowers, unfortunately no longer common, from cowslip to green-winged orchid, now rare. More generally, it is unusual these days to have the opportunity of seeing old-established meadows such as the Ings, and the great hedges, big enough to contain willow and even oak trees. We have lost very much permanent grass, very many hedges, and wildlife has suffered greatly. In arable fields without hedges there are no song posts for birds, fewer breeding sites and less cover. Weeds and insects have been killed off, mostly by chemicals; and ploughing up grassland has destroyed ant colonies, with the result that we have fewer green woodpeckers in Lincolnshire. The traditional mowing and grazing routine is followed at Bratoft Ings.

When you come to Bratoft church, you will find in the tower a painting on wood of the Spanish 'Armado' as a red dragon, with a doggerel inscription that merits a place in any anthology of bad verse:

> ". . . *This Dragon's guts, like Pharaos scattered hoast,*
> *Lay splitt and drowned upon the Irish coast.*
> *For of eight score save too ships sent from Spaine*
> *But twenty-five scarce sound return'd again*".

A different order of artistry is shown in the poppy-heads on the bench ends.

The Massingberd family lived at Bratoft but moved to Gunby in 1698. In Gunby's Victorian church there is a large brass to Sir Thomas Massingberd of about 1400 (and another Sir Thomas in 1522) as well as a rather smaller brass to William Lodyngton, Justice of the Common Pleas in 1419. When the Massingberds came to Gunby a hall was built for Sir William in 1700, the staircase and panelling (which are features of the interior) being added after 1735. Tennyson may have been thinking about Gunby when he wrote of 'A haunt of ancient Peace' in 'The Palace of Art'. Gunby Hall is now National Trust property, together with its 1,500 acres of grounds and the gardens.

The tall brick chimney of the Clover Milk Factory identifies Willoughby. The earliest farmers in the district have left round barrows, but ploughing goes on all around and all but over them. Near Burlands Beck, which flows past Willoughby, are remains of what used to be called a Danish camp but experts now decline to date them exactly. Willoughby is an example of a perimeter village, having had common land in the middle and houses built all round. The pattern, though considerably modified, can still be made out.

The Willoughby area is rich in characteristic Marsh names, including Ings, Grift—meaning a man-made drainage ditch, and Butterbump, which is our name for bittern (found occasionally at the nature reserve of Sea Bank Clay Pits, not far away).

The house where Willoughby's most famous son was born about

1580 can no longer be identified. He was John Smith, Captain John Smith of Virginia and of Pocahontas fame. The father, a tenant farmer, had property in Louth, where young John spent much of his schooldays. As a young man, Smith had an incredible series of adventures in fighting all over Europe, punctuated by a spell living alone in Tumby Wood near Tattershall. A year after its founding in 1606, the Virginia Company sent 105 colonists to Jamestown, and Smith was a member of the council. He soon became, through his capable, practical efforts, the mainstay of the colony. While exploring, he was captured by American Indians and saved from execution by 12-years-old Pocahontas. The later, sadder story of Pocahontas, la Belle Sauvage of so many inn signs, is also well known: how she consented to marry John Rolfe after being persuaded that Smith was dead, her journey with her husband to England, where she met Smith again, and her death from smallpox and burial at Gravesend in 1617.

Smith had returned to England in 1609, with the colony of Virginia securely established. In 1614 he successfully mapped parts of New England, including Massachusetts. This was his last expedition but he wrote much, fanning interest in the American colonies and providing advice for settlers. He died in 1631. There is no memorial to John Smith in his birthplace.

John Smith's first school was in Alford, the market town for the southern Marsh, as Louth is for the northern part. The market place is still crowded on Tuesdays, and especially for the annual cattle fair. Opening off the market place is West Street, where the buildings reveal eighteenth-century taste and prosperity. Lording it over West Street, and indeed the whole town, is the old Manor House, now Alford and District Civic Centre. A timber-framed building was erected about 1540, and this structure survives, though it cannot be seen. In the seventeenth-century brickwork was added to the H-shaped house. It is a picture when summer sunlight mellows the thatch and brick, and also in winter, with snow making smooth the roof but hardly powdering the two gables. A couple of farm waggons are preserved in the grounds behind the Manor. Alford almost rivalled Boston in contributing Lincolnshire settlers to the early North American colonies.

Like Burgh le Marsh, Alford has two windmills, one without sails, the other still working, as do only two others in the county. This Myer's mill, built in 1837, of six storeys, resembles the one at Burgh and the Maud Foster mill at Boston in having five sails.

One of the few recommended walks in the Marsh goes along a farmers' road known as the Two Mile Bank, from Gayton le Marsh to Theddlethorpe All Saints. According to tradition it was used by smugglers led by a parson, who told cottagers that any unusual sounds they might hear were made by the Devil and they should stay indoors and refrain from looking out. They did stay indoors, but the excisemen did not, and the gang was caught.

Theddlethorpe St Helen, of greenstone, in a setting of trees, with lovely grounds, has a fine stone reredos niche. So had Theddlethorpe All Saints, described by Pevsner as 'the richest of the churches in this Marshland . . . as varied in its architecture as in its furnishings'. It was known as the Cathedral of the Marsh. Alas, it is now closed.

I remember circling Theddlethorpe All Saints with a friend who, after speaking of the old barrel organ which it once had, talked about what can be done with such deserted churches. They could, of course, be pulled down and the stone re-used, but this is not economic, even if the stone is re-usable, which does not always follow. They could be turned into houses, except that the conversion is too expensive. In addition there is the problem of the graveyard's being consecrated ground. The fabric of Theddlethorpe All Saints is being maintained by the Redundant Churches Association, as a church, not as a museum, as was once planned.

Theddlethorpe has gained an oil terminal, well planned and not too obtrusive. Nearby is a magnificent ivy-covered farmhouse which I am tempted, like my friend, to regard as 'the best in Lincolnshire'.

Somewhat inland, South Somercotes is unusual in that its church has a spire, the only one in the Marshland. At a distance it obviously deserves its popular name of the Queen of the Marsh but I am not alone in feeling that close to, it is less impressive. Still, I readily join in the praise for the tower doorway and the three bells remarkable for their age—two of them are dated 1423—and for their excellent lettering (if you can see it after mounting all the steps of a ladder, for there is no stairway to the belfry). Emblems of the Passion are carved on the octagonal font, and the screen has several varieties of tracery.

Early last century five ships were wrecked on the coast, one of which was the *Rimac,* named after a river in Peru. There is Rimac House at one of the entrances to the Saltfleetby-Theddlethorpe Dunes National Nature Reserve, and hence many people call the reserve Rimac, not altogether with official approval.

The Saltfleetby reserve came into existence only after a series of events as strange as those which preceded the creation of the reserve at Gibraltar Point. In the 1920s a syndicate proposed to erect a garden city (or shack town, as opponents preferred to call it). Some buildings were put up by 1929. Lindsey County Council had plans to prevent the development, as they had saved Gibraltar Point, and prevent it they did—only to meet a setback. The land was taken over for practice bombing ranges along this part of the coast. That might be thought to end any hope of conserving the area with its birds and flowers and other features. However, all ended happily, with nearly 1,200 acres set aside as a reserve.

A great part of the reserve is in the danger-zone of firing ranges, and Royal Air Force safety regulations must be complied with; but the ranges are not used throughout the week. Strangely, the birds do not seem perturbed by the planes and the firing. Gulls and waders rarely bother to take wing even during practice explosions. Out in the sea are two pretty summerhouses on stilts, presumably not so much targets as landmarks for the flyers; they have, however, been destroyed from the air at least twice, and rebuilt.

In some respects Saltfleetby reserve resembles Gibraltar Point. The same expanses of sand and mud flats occur, the same process of colonisation by plants and the formation of salt marsh (at the northern end), the building of sand hills and the problems of dune erosion. Many species of birds are found in both reserves; redshanks, the first to give warning of an intruder; shelduck nesting in rabbit burrows; dunlin, ringed plovers and shorteared owl. The reserves likewise share many typical plants, including glasswort, Spring Beauty, dewberries with their greasy dull bloom and their failure to taste as sweet as they seem to promise, and notably formidable thickets of sea buckthorn. The female buckthorn has the bright

4 & 5. Two alabaster church monuments: John, Baron Willoughby (died 1372) in Spilsby and – reclining – Sir Adrian Scrope (died 1623) in South Cockerington

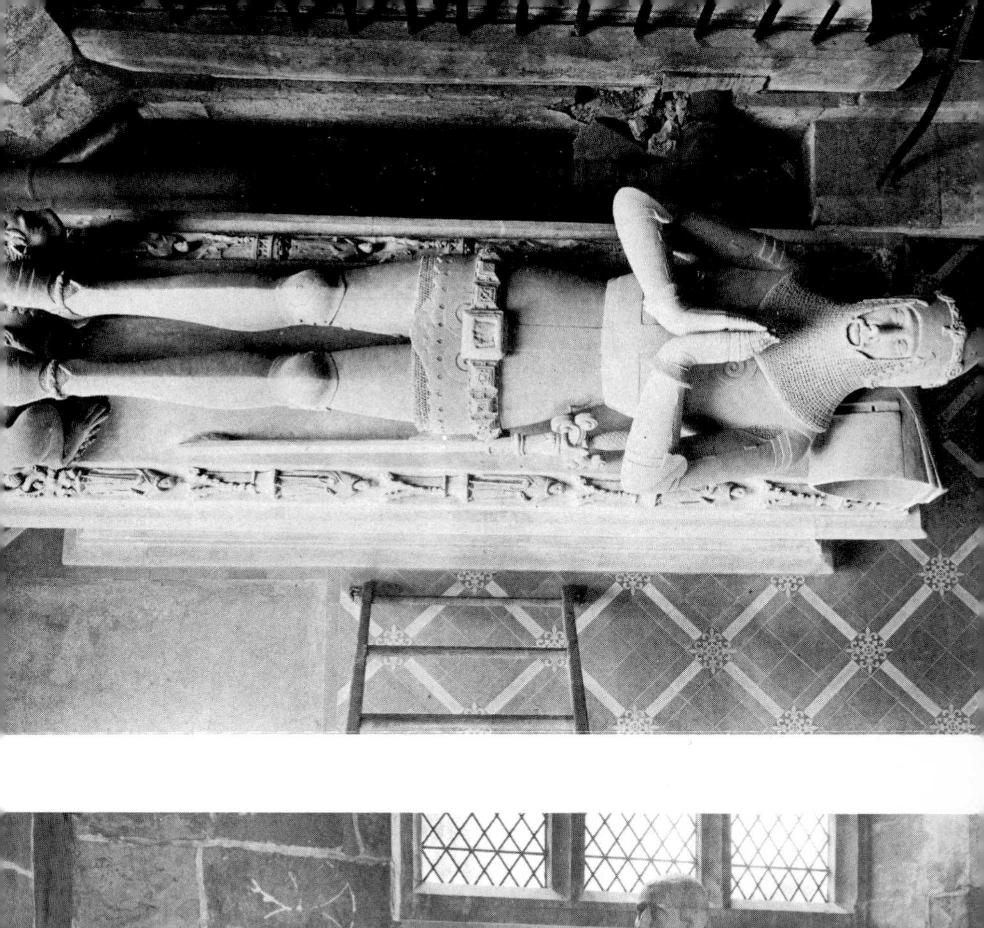

orange berries which make the shrub so attractive, not only to humans—the berries are the last source of food in a severe winter for such birds as fieldfares and mistle thrushes.

New dunes are being formed at the southern end of the reserve. Their longer-established neighbours naturally support a greater variety of plants, some of them colourful like viper's bugloss, and some rare like small meadow rue. The carline thistle and the pyramidal orchid are two somewhat unexpected plants to find in such a sandy habitat, for they like lime, but they can flourish here because fragments of seashells are abundant in the dunes.

The Saltfleet end of the reserve has a new salt marsh forming from silt deposited by the tide. Even before Domesday, Saltfleet was a port, though much afflicted by silting. Over the years the problem became so severe that about 1340 the Great Eau was diverted northwards to swell other streams which had formed Saltfleet Haven. This major effort failed to save the port.

Until 1340 the Great Eau's estuary was in what is now the reserve, near Rimac House. Today the old outfall is quite covered by a ridge of dunes. They were formed in the nineteenth century. They are some 150 yards farther east (towards the sea) than another ridge formed five centuries earlier. Between the two lines of ridges the beach has been converted by natural processes into a freshwater marsh.

This type of maritime fen is unique on the east coast of England. Bog pimpernel is one of the less common plants growing here, and there are two kinds of marsh orchid. A rarity of the freshwater marsh is the natterjack toad, which is not found elsewhere in Lincolnshire. It is distinguished by the yellow stripe down its back and by the fact that it does not jump but goes at a sprawling lope. These characteristics serve to identify the natterjack at a glance, but to see it at all is not very easy, for it generally feeds at night, lying up by day in sand burrows. The best chance of finding natterjacks is probably late spring, when numbers congregate to mate and spawn. Even then they are less likely to be seen than heard, the evening chorus of croaking males sometimes loud and distinctive.

No church exists at Saltfleet itself, though there used to be one, but it was washed away long ago—an ironic fate, considering that

6. *above* Tennyson's birthplace (1809), Somersby Rectory near Horncastle;
7. *below* Unfortified Norman manor house at Boothby Pagnell

the ancient port has been so thoroughly silted up. At Saltfleet nothing will shake the local conviction that Cromwell stayed here after the battle of Winceby (1643). He is supposed to have slept in the brick manor house, where some very early wallpaper, said to be the oldest in the country, has been preserved. The brick New Inn opposite is even bigger than the manor. Saltfleet has an association with Bonnie Prince Charlie, who came here in 1744 on a reconnaissance prior to his attempt in the following year to restore the Stuart dynasty. Saltfleet was one of the early eighteenth-century bathing places, and its sands are still popular in summer with visitors from nearby caravans, tents and chalets.

North of Saltfleet is Locksley Hall, a brick mansion originally from the sixteenth century, standing back from the road behind a lawn and surrounded by trees. I remember it in the thickening light of a cloudy summer evening through which the extraordinary collection of stained glass in the windows loomed dull purple. Under more favourable viewing conditions they are revealed as ranging from the Middle Ages to the present century, when an owner added to the saints, bishops and angels (one from the Bishop of Lincoln's palace at Buckden) and two panels from St Peter Mancroft, Norwich. Opposite, where Tennyson recalled how the Pleiads 'glitter like a swarm of fireflies tangled in a silver braid', are the lights and lightheartedness of the Lakeside Lido, with caravans and their tent supplements.

North again is yet another famous corner of the Lincolnshire coast, the evocatively named Donna Nook, another name taken from a wrecked ship. Do not be put off by the used-car dump on the way there, nor by the news that the authorities are considering transferring the bombing range here from Saltfleetby. The authorities have already decided to do away with the lifeboat station which did such valuable work here for so long. Now there is no lifeboat nearer than Spurn Head or Skegness.

At Donna Nook there is a coastguard station. The officers, I found, frequently marvel at the stupidity of people who venture too far out on the sands, despite warnings. The danger is very real. There is no spectacular frontal assault on the sand; the water flows round the shoals with bewildering speed, isolating a bar which is devoured at leisure—if that is the word for an advance which is so swift.

When the surges toss under a sky bruised by storm clouds, with hissing tattered waves boiling up beet-green, stories of wrecks and wreckers are only too plausible. A Mablethorpe man last century was reported as saying, 'Times are bad. But maybe the good Lord will send us a wreck'. Bodies of shipwrecked sailors are known to have been stripped at Theddlethorpe, and no doubt others met with similar treatment.

While an effort of imagination is required to conjure up any sympathy for the wreckers, few people have difficulty in admiring smugglers, known in Lincolnshire as owlers, from the hours they kept. The owlers took out wool and brought in contraband gin and unmanufactured tobacco. This free trade continued, with some variations, until almost yesterday. In fact, I sometimes wonder when anybody last looked (and what he saw) at the hooks in the roof of a drain tunnel near Huttoft from which contraband was slung. Many of the old facilities are evidently still available.

Heroes too are found on the Lincolnshire coast. Time after time men risked their lives to save the crew and passengers of stranded ships. Sometimes these brave men were those who under different circumstances acted as wreckers or smugglers. When possible, a boat was launched to the rescue, but on occasion local people have formed a human chain or ridden into the turmoil of the sea, swimming their horses part of the way to struggle through.

From Louth the river Lud runs, or at least makes its way, across the Marsh to its outlet in Grainthorpe Haven. When the Lud reaches Grainthorpe, formerly a port, it is within sight of the Georgian Hall and the brick-floored church which contains a much admired brass cross. Once the cross was longer than the fourteenth century rector whose monument it is, but now the stem has gone. The head, which remains, is beautiful, and the base rests on the depiction of a rock, sometimes said to be Golgotha, though it is set in a sea with fishes.

Because there is practically no stone in the Marsh, domestic buildings were mainly of brick, and most villages had their clay pits. You can see one by the roadside at Scupholme, for instance, and two at North Thoresby. The use of brick has produced some remarkable corkscrew chimneys, as at Saltfleet and on South View Farm, South Cockerington. The Marsh, incidentally, has a good share of moated houses. A fine example is Hanby Hall at Welton le Marsh in the south, and others are to be found near Withern, at Theddlethorpe St Helen and Scupholme.

The pre-Conquest villages were on the firm land, the clay; Fulstow is one. Out on the Marsh towards the sea, shepherds took advantage of islands or terraces to put up their cotes or sheep shelters, which formed the nucleus of such villages as North Coates and North and South Somercotes. The new villages reclaimed land around them, including coastal salt marsh. As land was available for peasants in the coastal villages, the Marsh became as densely populated as any region of Lincolnshire by Shakespeare's time. It has been suggested by Joan Thirsk that the development of the Marsh may have taken place at the expense of other areas in Lincolnshire; perhaps, for instance, causing the abandonment of some hamlets on marginal land in the Wolds.

Marsh Chapel, an offspring of Fulstow, has far outgrown its parent village. The Marsh Chapel church is big, Perpendicular in style if not as regards the axis of its tower, and untypically built of Ancaster stone, laboriously brought most of the way across Lincolnshire. Perhaps the parish could afford this status symbol because it became wealthy through the number of sheep on the reclaimed marsh (one gargoyle has a ram's head) and also through the medieval salt workings. A huge wooden bar secures the door of the church, where the Rurideconal Service is held on Ascension Day. The scale of the hospitality which traditionally follows makes it unlikely that those who attend can afterwards emulate Rupert Brooke's curates who 'come and go/On lissome, clerical, printless toe'.

A sight which has unfortunately become less common in the Marsh these days is the Lincolnshire Red shorthorn cow, a rather endearing beast, not smooth like a Jersey but somewhat rough, like much of the pasture that remains after the trend to arable farming. Some Lincolnshire Reds may, however, be seen on our way to Tetney.

Certain aspects of Tetney brand it as a dormitory of Grimsby but the place is worth examining. There is an excellent local history, published in 1901 by Rev. J. Wild, then Vicar. He traces the story from pre-Roman times. A hoard of Saxon coins was ploughed up in 1945. The Saxons built a church, but in 870 the Danes landed and are said to have burned it down, with much slaughter and cattle raiding. There are indeed fire marks on the walls of the church, though these walls are perhaps Norman.

By Domesday Tetney had thirteen salt works. Traces still remain—the circular hollows with a clay bottom, similar to those near Ingoldmells. As the sea retired, the Tetney salt works were more difficult to supply and the famous High Tide of 1571 all but destroyed them. In 1627 Sir William Carre of Sleaford substituted wild fowl for salt in payment of his Tetney rent. A salt road led up between Marsh Chapel and Grainthorpe towards the Wolds.

At Tetney in 1799 Arthur Young deplored the horrible neglect of the 'fine rich tenacious loam'. He saw 'a large open field in the fallow year . . . covered with thistles past their blossom, high enough to hide a jackass; yet the dung was spread amongst them as if the wheat could be sowed'. The enclosures came later to the Marsh than to most other regions of the county. Their heyday was from 1815-45, when more than half the enclosures of the Marsh were carried out.

After enclosure the soil and herbage of roads and lanes remained the property of the parishioners. The lanes were let by auction shortly after Easter each year, the highest bidder paying for one year's hire of them. The money was paid to the surveyor of highways and applied for various parish purposes. Some went to catching moles, some for cleaning ditches; the balance was generally claimed for the highway fund, but sometimes for the poor rate fund. The Tetney Parish Book records in 1818 'An Agreement entered into for the making and burning Bricks for the Roads. In this year £507.12.7½ was expended on the Highways'. Though it is not relevant, I cannot help quoting another entry, this time for 1845: 'A General Vestry summoned for February 6. Half past the time. Present, the Curate, 4 chairs and a form'.

At Tetney Haven the Louth Navigation reached the sea. The canal's route makes an interesting walk through the Marsh. Near its

end, the massive Tetney Lock is still to be admired, surviving since the Navigation was closed to shipping fifty years ago. The Lock is impressive even in decay. It is a favourite place for anglers. From there the canal went across a piece of marsh called Tetney Fitties. This ancient name denotes the outmarsh or land lying beyond the sea bank. Late in the Middle Ages the sea bank hereabouts is thought to be marked by the present road through North Coates, Marsh Chapel, North Somercotes, down past Saltfleet and Theddlethorpe St Helen to Mablethorpe. Locally at Tetney, as at many other places, it is known as the Roman Sea Bank, but old as it is, it does not date back as far as that.

For many people the most interesting feature of Tetney is its group of blow wells. These wells are formed by artesian springs where water under pressure escapes from the chalk through the overlying boulder clay to reach the surface. There are others at Barrow on Humber, and many more were present in the Marsh but most have dried up in recent years as the water table has been lowered by increasing abstraction.

The main wells can be reached by a path near the church. They are surrounded by grassland and separated by copses. Some of the trees are popular with thousands who have never been to Tetney, for they are willows which have yielded countless cricket bats. There are still traces of the old beds where watercress used to be grown. It is advisable to keep to the paths and not go too near the edge of the wells, which are unstable. The Lincolnshire Trust has a nature reserve by agreement with the Water Board, which has a pumping station there. The Board can count on a minimum two million gallons a day. The Trust can count on aquatic plants, birds such as snipe, reed bunting and sedge warbler, and pike and eels. The pike are supposed (not by the Trust) to grow to enormous size. This is not surprising, as the wells have long been claimed to be bottomless, or at least to run through to the Antipodes. The Trust allows them a depth of only 15 to 20 feet. That seems to rule out stories like that of a 'great lady, together with her coach and four', being swallowed in one and never seen again.

TWO

The Wolds

Along the Scarp

Being chalk uplands, and beautiful, the Wolds are often compared with the South Downs. Both areas are mainly treeless, with narrow valleys and steep scarps above extensive views, and both used to be largely given over to sheep-walks. The Wolds, however, are burlier, somewhat lacking the graceful swelling curves which lend elegance to the downland scene. They are some 45 miles long from north to south and anything from two to five miles wide—a sizeable plateau, highly irregular in outline and elevation. It is a more typically northern landscape than the Downs, one in which the beech is replaced by oak, ash and hazel, where any trees flourish, which is generally in the valleys; on the uplands the wind batters them awry, lichens enamel them green and gold, and in the thin soil they are stunted.

A lot can be learned about the Wolds by following a big empty lorry belonging to the North Lincolnshire Gravel Company as it swings down into Welton le Wold, a very pretty hamlet a few miles west of Louth. The lorry is going to fill up at a quarry. Here on the steep hillside a pheasant or two are stepping delicately, skylarks are singing, the cuckoo calls in summer, and below the green fields is the quarry. A sort of miniature Grand Canyon unexpectedly presents an extraordinary sequence of strata: a few inches of sandy top soil, then layers of chalk, at first white as mammoth bones which have been discovered at Welton, but lower down turning pink, and under that is red chalk.

Trees grow straight and tall on each side of the notch in which the hamlet lies. Prominent on a slope is a tall red brick house and under the square tower of the modern church is a house of whitewashed brick. The Wolds have stone, unlike the Marsh, but though chalk and sandstone were used, they are not good for building, so bricks were preferred. In the past the bricks were often whitewashed to resemble neighbouring buildings of chalk, and the custom lingers. Below the cottages a little stream emerges and flows alongside the road. This detail too is significant.

Like most Wold villages, Welton is in the valley, not because of the biting wind or from fear of the Danes, as has been suggested, but because on the upland there is no water. Up there, water seeps down through the chalk and only comes out as springs along the stratum of underlying boulder clay. Above the village houses, this spring-line can be clearly seen, marked by sedge tufts and often by churned-up mud where stock come to drink at a trough.

The Wolds have probably been colonised by farmers for as long as any other part of the county, the light soil being easy to work. The Romans built several villas on the fringes of the Wolds. The Angles are now only seen dead anywhere near the upland but when alive they certainly farmed here. The Danes came and settled in even greater numbers, and by Domesday the Wolds had the largest population of any region in Lincolnshire. Extensive sheep-walks date from at least the early Middle Ages, most of the wool going to Flanders and Italy through Lincoln, Boston and Hull. The coming of sheep has been said to result in the displacement of men from their mixed farms. The Black Death has also been blamed for economic hardship on the Wolds in medieval times. It may be that, as previously mentioned, the growing prosperity of the Marsh attracted settlers from the Wolds. At all events, farms were abandoned, and some entire villages.

One of the best known of these lost villages is Calceby, in sight of the road from Louth to Burgh le Marsh. It stood below a sloping hillside crowned by a chalk-built church which fell down 300 years ago. Looking down from the ruins on their knoll, it is easy to pick out the site of the village. Among some mounds in the pasture fields you can see the rectangular patches where houses had been built, and from their disposition it is possible to pick out faint traces of vanished paths between them.

It is less easy to see where other lost villages have been. At Cawkwell, for instance, on the road from Louth to Horncastle, a field falls steeply, like the road. In the field is all that remains of old Cawkwell, only a few blurred, random irregularities among thistles, sedge, mole hills and cattle tracks. Cawkwell once supplied Horncastle with water, which a century ago flowed there through a twelve-inch pipe from a spring that feeds the brook. Beside the spring is a font, brought there from Cawkwell church. That church must be one of the least visited in Lincolnshire. It stands—some of it, and only just—a few hundred yards away in an evil wood. The Sleeping Beauty cannot have been better protected than the church, which is embedded in a scarcely penetrable scrub, fiendishly barbed. A heavy stick is essential for beating a way through the massive brambles which smothered the tumbled gravestones. Only a few score strides in a direct line (which the undergrowth rendered impossible) separate you from the meadow, but in that fierce jungle you feel to be miles from civilisation.

There are other lost villages in the Wolds, some of them between the valleys economically named Poke Holes and Poke's Hole, and in other districts of Lincolnshire.

The western Wolds, which have the advantage of the picturesque steep scarp, are full of beauty spots as well as places of historical and other interest. One way of seeing them is to take the aptly named High Street. For once the Roman engineers allowed their hearts to rule their heads and adapted an ancient trackway for one of their more picturesquely sited roads. High Street follows the High Wolds south, seeming every now and then to be blown off course. Stretches of it are around 500 feet up, and it prefers the contours above 400 feet for miles. Steep ways drop down from it as it passes various Tops, a name given to high ground owned by the villages below. By Nettleham Top and Normanby le Wold the plateau reaches its highest level, nearly 550 feet. From here on the chalk you can look westwards to the limestone Cliff and, given the weather, to Lincoln cathedral. Long barrow builders were here, and Anglo-Saxons too, but lower down; their cemetery was discovered not long since. Some miles farther on, High Street rushes above Walesby, where a Roman villa, its hypocaust and household rubbish were found in 1861. Walesby has two churches, the older one as near High Street as possible. Its best known rectors were Robert Burton, author of the *Anatomy of Melancholy,* and Thomas Robert Malthus, the economist with controversial theories about population. The modern church in the village below was designed by Temple Moore in 1913.

Then there is Tealby, mounting by steps from the river Rase, which has been prettily bridged. Old-world cottages and their gardens remain among handsome modern houses and their carefully tended grounds. The manor was one of the 539 (76 in Lincolnshire) acquired by Odo, bishop of Bayeux, half-brother to the Conqueror, and derived its name of Bayons from the connection. Bayons Manor aroused the interest of Charles Tennyson, the poet's uncle. He added the name d'Eyncourt to his own and set about building a baronial home for himself, part manor house, part castle. The extraordinary medley was allowed to decay, and looked more extraordinary than ever, but in 1964 it was demolished with explosives and the park has been ploughed up.

High Street has several lofty miles more to go before it joins the road to Skegness through Horncastle.

The valley of the Bain is not to be missed. This little river, some twenty-four miles long—'clear Ban, the pretty brook', as Drayton called it—rises near Ludford and works its way south through Horncastle to join the Witham at Dogdyke near Tattershall.

Right on the edge of the Wolds is Hainton (though we leave the Bain to get there). It is more than 600 years since the Heneage family came to Hainton, where they have remained ever since. From the beeches on the main road the park stretches away, designed by Capability Brown in the 1760s. Hainton Hall was built in the seventeenth century, was extensively modified around 1807, when it was given stucco facing, and altered again in 1875. Capability Brown is thought to have built Hainton church spire during his work here. In the church are the series of Heneage monuments, some in the chancel, some in a chapel behind ornamental gates. There are floor brasses and wall brasses, inscriptions, tablets and busts, urns and effigies. The likenesses begin with a civilian, John Heneage (his brass goes back to 1435; his wife wears a horned head-dress) but many of his successors are in armour. Some Heneages recline, like black-bearded Sir George (1595), gilded, on his alabaster table tomb; others kneel, like his brother William (1610), also in alabaster. The family's links by marriage can be traced through the womenfolk: Skipwith, Cope, Fishbourne, Petre, Hunloke, Willoughby of Parham among them.

The grounds of a nineteenth-century yellow brick hall, Biscathorpe House, come down to the Bain and are the lovely setting for a nineteenth-century brick church. Biscathorpe church has long been a favourite picnicking spot. The church at Donington is not, for once, the main attraction. Donington water mill must be one of the most photographed places in the county, ranking with Lincoln cathedral, Boston Stump and Louth spire. In the foreground the little river is joined by a diversion which formed the mill stream, and where they come together a weir breaks flashes of white from them. This white seems placed with artistic skill, as on some lip in a Velasquez portrait, and is echoed in the calm reach of the mill stream which reflects the white fronted, white gabled, red roofed buildings flanked by trees.

Soon after crossing the abandoned railway track you have on your left a park containing a ruined old church, the park of the modern Stenigot House. Two alabaster tablets were brought from the old church to the new one on the edge of the park. The name on them is Guevara. Francis de Guevara was a Spaniard, a Protestant, who came to England when Katherine of Aragon did, and married and settled down here. His son John, who has the second memorial, was knighted after holding high office.

Taking the road on the opposite side of the valley to the RAF's huge radar dishes, you can climb up to the statutory nature reserve of Red Hill, mentioned briefly at the beginning of this book. Characterised by the red chalk we encountered at Welton, this reserve is a remnant of Lincolnshire's Wold downland. Apart from typical chalk plants, Red Hill is noted for its insects, butterflies and moths, and spiders. Common lizards are seen on the hillside, there is a badger sett, and this is one of the inland sites in Lincolnshire where the meadow pipit breeds.

You can leave the Bain once the valley broadens out, and return to Louth. There are many routes to choose from, and each has much to commend it. I like to work round by Raithby, where the church has a barrel organ. It has been flatteringly suggested that by following the working instructions, which have been preserved, anybody can play its thirty tunes. Several other churches besides Raithby and Theddlethorpe All Saints have or had barrel organs. These instruments replaced some church bands in the eighteenth and nineteenth centuries.

The last mile or two into Louth can be busy but apart from that they are delightful, ending by gliding down a pretty road with smooth high grassy banks between the traffic and the well kept gardens of suburban villas.

Louth

> Sleaford for sleep
> Boston for business
> Horncastle for horses
> Louth for learning.—Lincolnshire folk saying

Two Lincolnshire towns are often mentioned together for the general excellence of their architecture. One of them is the lovely stone-built town of Stamford; the other is Louth, made of brick. Louth has the advantage that (until today) its buildings have not been consciously preserved as works of art but remain because people have gone on living and working in them. Nobody would call Louth a museum of a town, for all that its centre has been declared a conservation area because of its historical and architectural merit. Half a dozen streets, satisfying in proportion and in details, demand to be lingered in. From a corner or down a tiny lane which somehow finds its way between shops and houses, an unexpected view of the wonderful steeple of Louth is suddenly revealed, the comparatively slender tower with its pinnacles joined by flying buttresses to the slender spire. Tower and spire are of the same height. The steeple has been compared with Boston Stump, with Grantham and with Salisbury. Local opinion is not alone in claiming that Louth should be preferred above them.

The steeple marks the pretty setting of Louth in its valleys at the edge of the Wolds. Coming from the south by the handsome upland road, or from the Marsh to the east, the spire shows up all of a sudden, beautiful and delicate. With it, another great building shows up, the huge malt kiln built in the 1950s to replace one that burned for days after German incendiary bombs hit it during the Second World War. The kiln is a good 140 feet high, the same height as the church tower without the spire. Many deplore the building of the kiln but there it is, and in fact it does not seriously challenge the steeple except from a few angles.

The atmosphere of Louth is best savoured on market days. The auctioneer's voice at the cattle market carries well but not quite across several streets downhill to Mercer Row, the main thoroughfare, now modernised but still retaining character. Off Mercer Row is the market place, the tall brick Market Hall and the Cornmarket. The old Corn Exchange building, which had a statue supposedly of Ceres halfway up its façade, was demolished in 1974. On market days the stalls all but hide the old shops and offices and the Masons' Arms, a renowned pub for townsfolk and farmers. At one end of Mercer Row is the King's Arms, a coaching inn where cock fights were held and where the Corporation met for a time in the eighteenth century, before the Freemasons made it their headquarters. At the other end is Parker's Bookshop, owned in 1827 by J. and J. Jackson, who published *Poems by Two Brothers,* namely Charles and Alfred Tennyson. Jackson is said to have made the authors take half their £20 fee in books and to have taught Alfred to smoke at the age of 12 by giving him a cigar.

The change in a street name exemplifies how life has gone on flowing through the same Louth channels for centuries. The name is Enginegate, formerly Lowgate. The ending gate is Danish and means 'way'. When the name was altered, the old ending was evidently considered too good to be lost even in the Industrial Revolution. Louth has many other -gates, from Upgate to Chequergate. In Eastgate there is the great Victorian Town Hall, several town houses and a modern shop bearing a sign informing you that the Greenwich meridian runs through Louth.

For admirable Georgian, Regency and Victorian houses the most notable street is Westgate, a testimony to Louth's good fortune in not having to depend on the prosperity of the Wolds alone but being able to draw on the wealth of the Marsh also. Markets and services, administrative business and the professions for a usually flourishing hinterland have been centred on the town for hundreds of years. Westgate is a grand street and has a grand pub, the Wheatsheaf, nobody knows quite how old but there is something that may have been a priest's hole above the bar. Off the street is a charming little alley with cottage gardens going down to the river Lud—Westgate Place, where Alfred Tennyson lodged during his unhappy years at the Grammar School (once in Westgate). At Westgate House, perhaps the outstanding mansion, a tesselated pavement was discovered during repairs in 1801, showing that the Romans paused in Louth as well as routing a road through it.

An Anglo-Saxon cemetery with 1,000 burials was uncovered at Acthorpe, South Elkington, on the outskirts of Louth, in 1947, and it is known that a party of Angles settled in Louth about the beginning of the sixth century. St Herefrid, abbot of Lindisfarne, later archbishop of Canterbury, is reputed to have founded a church in Louth and may have been buried there in 747. It was the Danes who made Louth a market centre and established its prosperity. Only seven Lincolnshire markets are mentioned in Domesday, of which Louth was one. From the time of the Norman Conquest until 1547 the Bishop of Lincoln was lord of the manor. In 1139 Bishop Alexander gave land in his park at Louth to Cistercian monks who had complained about conditions at their abbey at Haverholme, near Sleaford.

As usual with the Cistercians, the monks of Louth Abbey grew wealthy from the wool trade. Some wool was woven in Louth, but most of it was exported, at first by Flemings, later by Italians. Soon, with the aid of a loan from Aaron the Jew of Lincoln, the monks were able to build their abbey church of St Mary, seventy feet longer than the present St James's, the nave only a few feet narrower than that of Lincoln cathedral. King John may have stayed at the abbey when he passed through Louth in 1201 and again in 1216.

The town itself was prospering steadily. By 1276 a school was founded which became the Grammar School nearly three hundred years later. In Henry III's reign Louth was a serious rival to Lincoln and, with Sleaford, successfully resisted attempts to enforce membership of the Lincoln Merchant Guild. There was local rivalry too, directed against the abbey. Certainly Louth's growing wealth, including that of the guilds, and perhaps envy of the great church in Louth Park, seem to have decided the townsfolk to build a new parish church. Work on the new St James's was finished by 1441, not without setbacks, including shortage of money.

At this time there was a tower but no spire. That was begun in 1500 and finished in 1515, after more financial embarrassment. Stone was available at Donington on Bain but the famous Lincolnshire freestone was chosen, even though it had to be brought from Wilsford, Kelby and Heydour by water and waggon over forty miles of extremely bad roads. On the site the blocks were raised by a windlass formed of two ash trees from Thorpe Hall and two yew trees from the Park—the abbot gave one, but charged 3s 4d for the second, perhaps to show his resentment at this new threat to the pre-eminence of his own church. For the windlass 64 fathoms of cable from Lynn were sent by water to Ingoldmells and by land from there to Louth. The weathercock was made in Lincoln from a great copper basin, part of the booty taken from the Scots after the battle of Flodden.

So 'the last of the great parochial churches' was completed by the spire which William Morris said 'claims homage from the intellect as well as the imagination of man'.

While Louth church has been spared major disasters, some reconditioning has been necessary. It is tempting to believe that the storm in 1588 which blew down the weathercock was the same that routed the Spanish Armada. Repairs were undertaken in 1635, a third weathercock was erected in 1820, and the spire was once more mended in 1844, when a new top brought the height to one inch over 294 feet. The original apex was left in the rectory garden as a temporary measure but it is still there. Instead of Ancaster stone, the restorers used granite, which has darkened and now contrasts somewhat unfortunately with the rest of the spire. Guessing the size of the weathercock has led to some wild inaccuracies*. The last of

*King Cockerell is 18 inches high.

several further restorations was in 1936-37. Louth spire has been climbed several times (a trespassing offence), notably in 1818 by a man after he had downed ten pints of beer.

For all the praise lavished on the exterior of Louth's St James's, enthusiasm for the interior is often lacking. I am one of those who find it satisfying. The tower is open to a great height inside, and the eye is led up 86 feet to the roof. In the modern east window the glass is patterned so that a cross is discernible. What is most often deplored is the use of a modern alabaster font instead of the fine early fifteenth-century one brought from a garden. The woodwork, some of it modern, is of quality and includes the chest called the Sudbury Hutch, after the vicar who presented it before his death in 1504; and also another, seemingly made from an oak log. A row of eleven apostles is carved round the pulpit in detail extending to finger and toe nails; the twelfth—Judas—is represented below, as if he were in hell.

The carving is the work of the Lincolnshire Gibbons, otherwise Thomas Wilkinson Wallis, born at Hull in 1821 but spending much of his long life in Louth. He worked at first for a drunken gilder, whom he succeeded when the man died in 1844, the result (it was firmly believed even in those Victorian times) of his having been bewitched by a local wizard. Wallis started wood carving in 1850, then 23 years later he turned to surveying because his eyesight was no longer good enough for fine work. He became Borough Surveyor in 1885 and died in 1903, known as a botanist, naturalist and geologist in addition to his reputation in other fields. Wallis persisted in admiring James Fowler, the Louth restorer of many churches, frequently criticised by others; and carved his head near the organ. As a surveyor, Wallis excavated Louth Abbey, of which so little remains.

The fortunes of the Abbey had declined after the Black Death and it was dissolved in 1536, the roof pulled down, its lead stripped off, the bells broken up and the valuables carted away. Similar events took place all over the country but in Lincolnshire they had exceptional consequences. At Louth, for special reasons, a protest movement began in September 1536, leading to what is often called rebellion against Henry VIII's policy, though not against the king.

8. *above* Fulbeck, claimed as the prettiest village in Lincolnshire; 9. *below* Bourne church, all that remains of the Norman abbey

It so happened that Louth and district were being visited by several groups of officials who aroused suspicion, fear and resentment. People were afraid that the valuable church plate would be handed over and their feelings about this and about the actions of the King's Commissioners were roused by the Vicar, Thomas Kendall, a shoemaker, Nicholas Melton, generally considered to be the leader soon known as Captain Cobbler, a former monk at Louth Abbey, William Moreland, and about fifty local clergy whose fitness for office was being tested by the Commissioners.

Another set of King's Commissioners were in the district, these charged with assessing the subsidy granted by Parliament. Hearing that they would be in Caistor, Melton decided to go and meet them. He set off at daylight with a large following, including Moreland, and compelled the Commissioners to join the movement. However, one of them, Lord Borough of Gainsborough, escaped and sent word to the king. The gentlemen captured at Caistor included Sir Robert Tyrwhit, who with the others signed a letter to be taken to the king at Windsor by Sir Edward Maddison and John Heneage. Another letter was sent to Lord Hussey, the lord lieutenant, at Sleaford, telling him to come and aid the commonwealth or be regarded as an enemy.

By now the movement had spread widely through the county. It was obvious that to succeed in the march on Lincoln now decided, the people must organise, and at Louth various town groups were formed into companies. Disturbances had occurred at Spilsby, Market Rasen, Boston and Lincoln, but most violently at Horncastle. After mustering, the people set off for Market Rasen and then for Lincoln, joined on the way by men from Kirton, Boston and Horncastle. The force numbered perhaps 100,000 but some went very reluctantly and for the first time there was a suspicion that the gentry would betray the commons. The gentry urged patience, the commons wanted to move on to Newark and link up with supporters from Hull and Halifax.

Lord Hussey made no move. The Earl of Shrewsbury, supposed to be acting for the king, decided he could do little, so remained at Nottingham. Meanwhile Henry VIII, impatient and not a little frightened, appointed Charles Brandon, Duke of Suffolk, as com-

10. Swans in 'The Glory Hole' under High Bridge, Lincoln

mander-in-chief. Brandon had married a de Eresby heiress, and Eresby House at Spilsby had been attacked, so the king no doubt thought that Brandon would act vigorously against the 'rebels'. As a matter of fact, Brandon had some sympathy with them and needed further royal prompting.

Before he could take the field, however, the movement collapsed with surprising speed. Great numbers of people had begun to leave Lincoln as dissension grew between gentry and commons. The gentry had no heart for opposition involving high treason. The commons hesitated to take up arms against the king. There was a tense moment when a letter from the king was read by Thomas Moyne to a gathering in the Chapter House at Lincoln and he omitted 'a little clause' whereupon, he reported, 'a parson from Snelland said the letter was falsely read and I was like to be slain'. He was smuggled out while further action was debated—and none taken. The 'little clause' would undoubtedly have worsened the situation if it had come to the ears of the people it described as 'the rude commons of one shire and that the most brute and beastly of our whole realm'. But it was not made public and next day the gentry, armed now and backed up by their retainers, informed the commons that they would take no further action until they had a reply to another letter they had written to the king. At this, Melton said, 'the commons stole away apace'. Two days later the rebellion was over, after less than a fortnight. Suffolk rode into Lincoln unopposed.

The vicar of Louth, William Moreland and other leaders went into hiding but all were taken, except perhaps Captain Cobbler, about whose fate we know nothing. Six men were executed and hung up in Louth on a market day. Others put to death were monks from Kirkstead, Barlings and Bardney abbeys. Only a somewhat reluctant participant named Robert Aske found his way to Yorkshire and was forced to lead the movement known as the Pilgrimage of Grace. This title is not applied to the Lincolnshire movement which began at Louth and had the same objects. Louth Abbey was given to Lord Borough but was soon acquired by the Duke of Suffolk to add to the 22 monastic sites he had already received.

In 1551 a charter was given to the newly named but already

ancient Edward VI Grammar School. It moved to Schoolhouse Lane, off Goose Pool Gate (now Gospelgate), where there is a statue of the 'founder', but the building became part of the Girls' Grammar School, and since 1930 the boys have a new school in its own grounds. The old Grammar School had John Smith (of Virginia) and John Franklin, as well as Tennyson, among its pupils.

Louth has strong associations with Australia through the school. The explorer Edward John Eyre was a scholar from 1830-31. Two years later Eyre went to New South Wales and spent some time adventurously shifting stock overland to Adelaide and Melbourne before turning to exploration. It was his third expedition which brought him renown. In 1840 he headed a party aiming to find a route from Adelaide to the north. On a terrible journey, his discoveries included the lake named after him. Later, Eyre became lieutenant governor of New Zealand and then went to the West Indies. While he was governor of Jamaica in 1865 there was rioting and Eyre's rigour in suppressing the disturbance was condemned as unduly severe, though he was officially commended for initiative.

Contemporary with Eyre at Louth Grammar School was Augustine Charles Hobart-Hampden, third son of the Earl of Buckinghamshire, a character as picturesque as Captain John Smith. A sailor, he fought Brazilian slavers, then served in the Baltic during the Crimean War. When the American Civil War broke out, he commanded a ship, as Captain Roberts, and underwent many adventures while several times breaking the Northern blockade of the Confederate states. After this poaching experience, so to say, he turned gamekeeper under the Turkish Sultan and foiled Greek blockade-runners to Crete. As Hobart Pasha he had command of the Turkish Fleet in the Black Sea.

In the eighteenth century Louth became one of the liveliest centres in the county. The Mansion House in Upgate was called the Assembly Rooms, and residents and visitors patronised the gatherings, masquerades and concerts. The social life led some clergy to abandon their parishes and move into Louth. John Wesley often came to Louth, not so much for the festivities as to preach and to call on his sister Hetty, who lived there for a while after her unhappy marriage. Later, Byron paid a visit to the town; and in 1825 Madame

Tussaud brought her exhibits to the Mansion House (which became the Mechanics' Institute in 1853).

From 1770 until 1924 Louth was a port, thanks to the canal known as the Louth Navigation, connecting the town to Tetney Haven. Ships of thirty tons could come up to the river basin, doing much trade in coal, corn and wool. Riverhead is still an interesting place to look round, with old wool and carpet factories in James Street. Wool was washed in the river and spread out on the banks to dry. For a generation after the coming of the railways the canal survived, with a weekly trading service to Grimsby and Hull, and monthly to London. To get into the canal from the sea, ships had to take a favourable tide. This could cause inconvenience to the boatmen and their families, who often went on the voyages. It is not long since a Riverhead character died at an advanced age, who claimed to have 'lived in this house all my life'. Asked if he was born there, he replied no, but he came when he was four days old. He had been born on a ship that had to wait for the tide, but the baby would not wait to be born and so his birthplace was officially recorded as 'at sea'. With the extension of the railway to Lincoln in 1876 and to Mablethorpe in 1877, the canal's usefulness dwindled.

In turn, Louth railway station has been closed. The nearest railhead is 14 miles away at Market Rasen. To get there is easy if you can afford a taxi; if not, not, for there is no bus service. No premonitions seem to have clouded the opening ceremony at the station in 1847, when the foundation stone was laid by Miss Charlotte Alington Pye, who became a Victorian celebrity as composer of such songs as 'Come back to Erin', under the pseudonym of Claribel.

Claribel's father was involved in a sorry scandal. Born Henry Alington in 1799, he took the surname Pye after benefiting from the will of a distant relative in Cheshire. He was a solicitor, a local dignitary, member of Louth Corporation, for instance, and County Treasurer for Lindsey. His house, now 25 Gospelgate, was used as the County Court, as the arrangement of the rooms and the presence of an enormous wall safe still show. In 1868 Pye's friend and partner was declared bankrupt and soon Pye was considering suicide or flight, for he had been using the County Treasurer's fund to meet private debts. Having decided to flee, Pye saddled a horse and galloped away just as the police broke in. He tried to row across the Humber at the age of 68, with only one leg (the other lost in an accident). For at least three days he was on the water, then was picked up and managed to reach London. Claribel joined him and they decided to go to Belgium, where he lived until 1882 as an undeclared outlaw. Claribel lived only a year. Pye's second wife, Lady Albinia Frances Hobart, daughter of the Earl of Buckinghamshire who had extensive estates in Lincolnshire, lived on until 1885.

A cloudburst over the basin of the Lud in 1920 sent floods of water down the valley, turning the pretty stream above Louth into a destructive torrent two hundred yards wide. Near Riverhead three cottages dammed the onrush, which very quickly rose more than twenty feet before the obstruction was swept away. A score of people were drowned, many houses were wrecked, many more damaged and polluted by the mud that remained after the flood had subsided.

The storm water had built up in Louth's natural park, a very delightful glen called Hubbard's Hills, named after an eighteenth-century resident and donated to the town by August Alphonse Panud, a master at the Grammar School early this century. From one rim of the little gorge the trees slant down to meadows embellished by the 1937 Jubilee plantations. The other side of the valley consists of chalk cliffs where beech trees have astonishingly sprung up and flourished in shallow soil on the steep slope. Hubbard's Hills make an agreeable promenade for townspeople coming there past the water mill at the lower, less precipitous end of the valley.

Fronting Hubbard's Hills is Thorpe Hall, said to have been built in 1584 by Sir John Bolle. Sir John served with the Cadiz expedition of 1596 and was knighted for valour. Several well-born hostages were taken and an almost contemporary ballad recounts how one Spanish lady fell in love with a gallant English captain, identified as Sir John Bolle. In 1592, however, he had married Elizabeth Waters of Kings Lynn, and he was a faithful husband. To the grief of the Spanish lady, Sir John courteously rejected her advances. Donna Leonora Oviedo, if that really was her name, sent her portrait in a green dress and a gift of jewels for his wife, then retired to a nunnery and, as far as we know, died there.

Ownership of Thorpe Hall passed from the Bolles, but no matter what family was in possession or in residence, the ghost of the Green Lady has been reported haunting the gardens right up to a few years ago. Until the 1920s a place was set for her at the dinner table in case she decided to appear.

Adequate accommodation is much easier to find in Louth than in some other Lincolnshire places. Recent experience up and down the county prompts the generalisation that private hotels and guest-houses have improved their comfort, food and service enormously, which is unfortunately not true of many hotels. The matter of accommodation is emphasised because Louth is such an excellent centre for touring the Wolds and much of Lincolnshire.

The Eastern Wolds

The eastern area of the Wolds rivals that on the west. From Louth we can thread through byways to the entrancing village of Little Cawthorpe. Here the water course known as the Long Eau rises from springs which form a pond and the stream flows down as Watery Lane. The rivulet is actually the road and is used as such by horses, carts, lorries, tractors and sometimes cars, as shown by the tracks in its bed. It is thoughtfully marked 'Unsuited for light motor vehicles' and you can cross it by a water splash. Some trout used to live in the stream but as they were known individually by name, nobody dreamed of trying to catch them.

There is, however, 'Trout's Leap' at Little Cawthorpe. You leave the village, its stream, pond, hall and church by a sunken lane, perhaps fifteen feet wide, its sides steep and hedged. Local people say it has not changed appreciably since the day in 1866 when, for a wager, Dr Trought (or Trout), a mayor of Louth, put his horse at this alarming obstacle and cleared it.

It is no hardship to join the main road to Skegness for a spell, despite a good deal of holiday traffic, for it climbs to about 300 feet and rushes along for miles at about this height. The section I like best is where it drops into Burwell valley after passing quite extensive woods on the edge of the Wolds. The Church Hall at Burwell is an octagonal brick building under a conical roof and a cupola, which used to be the Butter Market when Burwell had a market, and then a dovecote.

A couple of miles farther on, at Walmsgate, watch out for a grove of trees just north of the road. It is Beacon Plantation, where a great heap of wood soaked in pitch was kept during the Napoleonic wars to be set alight as a signal in case of invasion. The trees mark but do not hide the biggest long barrow in Lincolnshire. It is nearly 260 feet long, about 65 feet wide and still stands higher than a man at the broad end, towards the road, in spite of having been robbed of a good deal of its stone.

We must turn off the main road to find Swaby, one of the most interesting of Wold villages. In the church, with luck, there will be an explanatory leaflet, a model of its kind. Much of the information in it applies to the Wolds in general, although of course the main emphasis is on the story of the people who lived at Swaby.

Flint axe-heads are still occasionally discovered in the fields, while in 1933 a hoard of Roman coins was ploughed up and later presented to Lincoln Museum. Swaby is a Danish name, the village of Svafi, but Pado Lane in the village was originally Pays d'Eau, referring to the meadows beside Swaby beck. From 1350 to 1951 Magdalen College, Oxford were patrons and they still own much of the land.

The present church of St Nicholas replaced a previous one, described as 'small and sordid', and a still earlier church on the same site is known to have existed. Violins and clarinets were used at the services until about 1900, when an organ was brought from Haugh Manor. The east window is now one sheet of clear glass, beyond which are trees, so the worshippers seem to be in a glade. Another contemporary feature is the hanging glass cross. Once a month the service is conducted in the Methodist tradition, and occasional united services are held with the neighbouring parishes of South Thoresby and Belleau-with-Aby, which share the same Rector. Swaby has a tradition of tolerance for dissenters, including Anabaptists as early as 1690. In 1866 a Wesleyan chapel was built to serve villages where the squires would not permit such development; the chapel has been closed, part of it serving as the Village Hall, the rest for storage.

Pinfold Hill is a reminder of the time of open field cultivation. There the Pinder collected all the animals grazing on the common pasture and the owners had to reclaim them with a fee. That was changed at the end of the eighteenth century, for an enclosure act for Swaby and Belleau was passed in 1791. For the next seventy years the population increased, reaching nearly 500. There were 115 children in the school; three inns on the main road, presumably as a staging post between Louth and Spilsby; and three shoemakers in the village. Then more arable farming came to be practised and at the same time a steady migration to the towns took place. Now there are about 160 inhabitants, under 40 children in the school, no inns and no shoemakers.

The White Pit near Swaby was a chalk quarry. Some of the older houses are built mainly of chalk but its principal use was for roadmaking. In 1860 a ninepenny rate was levied, providing £61, all of it used for the upkeep of the highways. To maintain the beauty of the Wolds, the parish council of Swaby arranged in 1970 for their land at White Pit to be planted with beech, sycamore, whitebeam and maple, setting an example for other villages to follow.

We can follow lanes to Belleau, which was recorded in Domesday as Elgelo and later became Hellow. Springs bubble out between chalk and clay, forming a pond and going to swell a tributary of the Great Eau. Opposite the pond is an octagonal pigeon cote built of small bricks, with a slate roof, and a big damp patch on one wall. White-throated house-martins are often seen darting round it. Down the lane is Belleau Manor, moated, also of brick but not as old as one of its barns, thought to have been part of a house belonging to the Willoughby de Eresby family. On another building (modern) is the bust and bearded head of a wild man. He is a Wodewose, a creature who in Gothic times held the imagination as the satyr did during the Renaissance. More than two hundred European families—including the Willoughbys—had a Wodewose in their emblems. Part man, part animal, savage and erotic, he was supposed to arouse fear and envy.

Sir Henry Vane the younger took over Belleau manor from the Willoughbys. This Sir Harry Vane sailed to Massachusetts in 1635 on board the *Abigail,* and the following year became governor.

During his term of office Harvard was founded. Vane returned to England, served the Commonwealth during the Civil War but retired to Belleau after marrying the daughter of Sir Christopher Wray of Barlings. Charles II decided that Vane was guilty of treason and regrettably had him executed. American as well as English admirers of Sir Harry Vane subscribed to the memorial placed in Belleau church in 1915.

Unless you look for it, Haugh could be overlooked but should not be. It is perched high up on a bleak moorland ridge and consists principally of a Tudor manor house with a big chimney stack, and a tiny church, partly of chalk, without tower or spire. The interest, apart from Norman features in the church, is the connection with the Bolle or Bolles family. Originally the Bolles came from Bolle Hall at Swineshead, and there are other Fenland associations, as also with Saltfleetby All Saints, Scampton and Elsham. In Haugh church an alabaster tablet with coat of arms recalls Charles Bolle, who married a Dymoke lady from Scrivelsby, then two other ladies in succession and fourthly a Dymoke bride from Friskney. His son, Sir John Bolle, has a more elaborate alabaster monument. He was the gallant English captain with whom the Spanish lady fell in love, the builder of Thorpe Hall at Louth.

From Haugh we go back to the main road at Miles Cross Hill, once a sea cliff, then several million years later covered by a glacier which scoured it into a smooth slope, made even smoother several thousand years after that by highway engineers. A lane brings us to the wooded valley of Well Vale, reaching back into the Wolds, and to the magnificent gates of the park surrounding Well Hall, or Wellvale House, as it is also known. Assuming that the gardens are open, we drive slowly past the great trees and string of lakes (fishing by permission) to the Georgian house, its front slightly asymmetrical, as all human faces are. From the house we can walk to the Georgian temple of a church. Inside, the stucco ceiling, the pews arranged sideways and the three-decker pulpit distract attention from a very odd feature: the altar is not at the east end of the church, but the west. The tale goes that the architect made a blunder about the position of the altar and when it was pointed out was so mortified that he shot himself. This is not now generally believed. Another explanation is that the unusual position of the altar was chosen so that worshippers (then mainly guests) could admire the view from the east entrance: the Hall, its ornamental water to the left, the landscaped garden, the beech trees, all very attractive, if stage-managed.

At the sight of a great bronze man standing near the western end of Spilsby the road divides into two, forming the market place. The bronze man is Sir John Franklin, Spilsby's best known son, unless we award the palm to Victor Sylvester, the band leader. Monday is market day and has been for more than six hundred years, the day when a man could buy or sell a wife—at least until the eighteenth century, when the going price was ten shillings. The stalls of that period, or some of them, were set up under the five arches on which the building which was then the Town Hall still stands in the market place behind Franklin's statue. At the far end, to the east, is the Butter Cross, dating from the fourteenth century.

On one side of the market square is the White Hart, a coaching inn with a very old stone letter box in the wall beyond a bay window. Not far away a house was built over what used to be called Jenning's Smoot, a name relinquished in favour of Franklin Passage, for the house was where John, the youngest of twelve Franklin children, was born in 1786. He had a varied and distinguished career, including naval service, exploring Australia and then the Mackenzie River basin in northern Canada, and acting as governor of Van Diemen's Land (Tasmania), before leaving in 1845, when nearly 60, to try to discover the North West Passage. None of his company in the *Erebus* and *Terror* returned. Two older brothers distinguished themselves in India: Major James Franklin carried out the first military survey in India, and Sir Willingham became a judge in Madras.

Some unusual fourteenth-century alterations to Spilsby church turned what was the chancel into a chapel. In the chapel are remarkable monuments to members of the Willoughby de Eresby family.

The first of the monuments is the tomb where John, Baron Willoughby de Eresby, who fought at Crecy, lies cross-legged, his wife Joan with him. Next in time is his heir, also John (1372), standing in alabaster, who was at Poitiers. Robert (1396) and his third wife, Elizabeth Neville, are in alabaster too, but lying; Robert's second wife, Margaret Zouche, has a large brass. Under canopies there are brasses almost as big as hers to William and his first wife, Lucy Zouche. Grandest of all, practically filling the wall of the chapel, is the massive and elaborate stone screen commemorating Richard Bertie (1582) and Katherine, Baroness Willoughby de Eresby, whom he married in 1553. Their alabaster busts stand in niches, with a leaf-clad Wodewose among the three figures standing over them.

Katherine was the only child of William, Lord Willoughby, who in 1516 married Mary de Salinas, a Spanish lady, cousin of Katherine of Aragon. As a fatherless child, Katherine Willoughby was Baroness in her own right and became the ward of Henry VIII, who sold the wardship to his brother-in-law, Charles Brandon, Duke of Suffolk, for £2,266 13s. 4d. Suffolk married Katherine when she was sixteen. Richard Bertie was her second husband, whom she preferred to a royal suitor, the King of Poland.

Bertie and Katherine were Protestants and went abroad to avoid persecution during Mary Tudor's reign. Their son, Peregrine Bertie, Lord Willoughby de Eresby, was born during their exile. Under Elizabeth I he became famous as a military leader, his exploits being celebrated in 'The ballad of the brave Lord Willoughby'. Peregrine Bertie died in 1601. On his Spilsby monument he stands, armoured and very erect, in a recess and below him lies his only daughter, Katherine Lady Watson, who died in childbirth in 1610. And that is the end of the Willoughby monuments in Spilsby church. Another series, however—the greatest in Lincolnshire—graces Edenham church, the manor of Grimsthorpe having been granted to the Lord Willoughby who married Mary de Salinas, the then queen's cousin. Eresby Hall at Spilsby ceased to be the Willoughby seat, and it was destroyed by fire in 1769.

The road from Spilsby to Horncastle climbs to an exposed whaleback ridge at Winceby. To the north a track leads through a deserted churchyard to the nature reserve of Snipe Dales (public access). The first impression is of moorland with rough grass falling steeply into a valley which is soon seen to be a complex of tiny dales and their becks. Botanists I have accompanied to Snipe Dales were enthusiastic about the succession of vegetation from the high ground down to the spring-line and lower still to marshy areas. In one place I found some feathers and other pheasant remains near a fox's earth, with a badger's sett only a few feet away. Voles abound, preyed on by short-eared owls and kestrels, and apart of course from snipe, there are woodcock and heron, and a colony of sand-martins.

It is a long slog back up through the tufts of grass and sedge, and we paused thankfully near the old gravestones among brambles and ivy in the deserted churchyard. Westwards, the plateau is cut up into a number of valleys. Through them Cromwell's Roundheads pursued their routed opponents in October 1643. This battle, which began at Slash Lane, was nearly Cromwell's last. He had ordered an immediate charge but his horse was killed and while he was on foot he was knocked down by a blow from Sir Ingram Hopton. Before he could press his advantage, however, Hopton was caught in the onrush, Cromwell mounted another horse and joined a second charge. In less than an hour the King's forces were shattered. The defeat was one of the factors which turned the scales against the Royalists.

Hopton was killed at Winceby. Cromwell slept the night in Horncastle, though not at Cromwell House in West Street. He arranged for Hopton to be buried in Horncastle church, where there is a memorial painting to him. Also in the church are a dozen scythe blades, said to have been used at Winceby or in the religious unrest of 1536. The church has a brass to Sir Lionel Dymoke (1519), the King's Champion, of the family we shall hear more about at their seat, Scrivelsby. In a case is a collection of chained books, including an early edition of *Foxe's Book of Martyrs.*

Near the church is a section of Roman wall, and another section can be seen at the Library. The Roman name of Banovallum is no longer considered correctly applied to Horncastle, though the Romans did enclose several acres. Coins from Vespasian's reign (*c.* AD 78) and Severus Alexander's (*c.* AD 222) have been found, and I heard that a Horncastle man discovered a Roman building under his front garden nearly thirty feet down, though I don't know what gardening technique requires digging to such a depth.

The present name of the town seems derived from Hyrn-ceaster, the camp at the horn—a reference to its situation on a peninsula or horn between the rivers Bain and Waring. In the eighteenth century Horncastle had its canal, now disused, but the basin in the centre of the town is a pleasant place, with a big old warehouse still standing, and trees on both sides.

There are Banks Street and Banks Road, named after Sir Joseph Banks of Revesby, a grandee of many parts, as we shall learn in due course—who had a town house in High Street and who sponsored a public dispensary in 1789. As might be expected, Woolworth's is centrally placed, occupying the site of Sellwood House, home of two nieces of Sir John Franklin, one of whom, Emily Sellwood, married Alfred Tennyson after a long engagement. The smallest building I know of in Horncastle is the tiny place whose eaves I think (wrongly) I can touch—the shoemaker's shop that belonged to William Marwood, hangman.

Until last century the August horse fair at Horncastle was the biggest in England. George Borrow wrote of his encounters there in *The Romany Rye.* The horse fair has gone, and the market is no longer held in the street, which is no longer cobbled. Doctors used to put straw over the cobbles to deaden the noise. There is still noise from holiday traffic to and from the coast.

South of Horncastle a pleasant road east of the highway has a section between trees where there are two lodges attributed to Humphry Repton next to park gates which bear a stone lion. He is the Scrivelsby lion, replacement of one set up around 1530 by Robert Dymoke, Hereditary Grand Champion to Richard III, Henry VII and Henry VIII. The King's Champion, it will be remembered, officiated at the Coronation, riding fully armoured into Westminster Hall and throwing down his gauntlet as a sign he was ready to fight any person who questioned the king's right to succeed. The king gave the champion a gold cup, several of which are preserved at Scrivelsby. The last coronation at which the picturesque challenge was made was that of George IV in 1821. Following a modern custom, the present Champion carried the Standard of England at Elizabeth II's coronation.

The Dukes of Normandy had as their hereditary champion a

member of the Marmion family. A Marmion naturally accompanied William the Conqueror. This Marmion, Robert, was made King's Champion and given the manor of Scrivelsby (and that of Tamworth). In 1350 the Marmion line died out and the estate and title passed to the Dymoke family (the name is pronounced 'Dimmock'). Ever since Richard II's time, therefore, a Dymoke has been Champion.

Scrivelsby Park, for long sheltering fallow deer, was laid out by Humphry Repton at the end of the eighteenth century, but Scrivelsby Court has been demolished. The former gatehouse has been converted into a residence, not as much of a come-down as might seem.

Monuments in Scrivelsby church to past champions begin with a cross-legged effigy generally identified as that of the last of the Marmions. Sir Robert Dymoke (1545), builder of the Lion Gate, has a tomb with a brass effigy on the lid. Brass tablets commemorate the Champion to James II, Sir Charles Dymoke (1686), who fell full length on approaching the king, and George III's Champion, John Dymoke. Standing against the wall is the marble memorial and bust to Lewis Dymoke, Champion to George I and George II. Like the Tudor Sir Robert who lived under five kings and officiated for three of them, this Lewis Dymoke survived to an advanced age, dying in 1760 when he was 90.

South of Scrivelsby, the main road to Skegness can be jammed with holiday traffic. A charming détour to Bolingbroke, however, can be made along delightful byways. Soon hedge parsley will be brushing the car on either side. Gates shut off a field where grazing cows pretend that nothing is farther from their intentions than to make off if the gates should be left open. The fields are vivid green, sprinkled with the simple flowers that Chaucer loved. In the hedges are other English flowers, including dog-rose and honeysuckle. The countryside is bosomy, heaving gently, the lanes loop up and down, to and fro, with an occasional dragonfly-dart at the top of a knap. In the few tiny hamlets are rewarding churches, fine manor houses and glorious views across the enchanting countryside.

At Bolingbroke there are Lancaster roses outside the Black Horse Inn, symbol of John of Gaunt. The first Bolingbroke castle was built by William de Roumare, Earl of Lincoln, the earliest Norman to hold the title. John of Gaunt married his cousin Blanche, heiress of the Earl of Lancaster, and thereby acquired Bolingbroke, where he came to live and where in 1367 a son was born who took the title of Bolingbroke and later the crown of England as Henry IV.

Gaunt was a patron of Geoffrey Chaucer, who strengthened the link about 1366 by marrying Philippa Rouet, sister of Katherine de Rouet of Hainault, first the wife of Sir John Swynford of Kettlethorpe, then Gaunt's mistress and, in 1396, his third wife. The Duchess Blanche had died of plague in 1369, and Chaucer honoured her memory in an early poem, 'The Deth of Blaunche the Duchesse'. Chaucer is believed to have visited Bolingbroke on several occasions.

John of Gaunt built most of the greenstone church and enlarged the castle to make it more conveniently habitable. When Cox wrote in 1924 only 'some mounds and a few basement courses' were visible but on my last visit the layout was taking shape as excavations continue. The castle had been reduced by Parliamentarian forces in the Civil War, when it surrendered after the battle of Winceby in 1643. Parts of it stood for long afterwards but 'the last standing remains . . . crumbled over their base last week and came to the ground', as the *Gentleman's Magazine* reported in May, 1815.

The village is quaint and rewarding, and indeed was justly made a Conservation Area by Lindsey County Council. Beyond the pond, house-martins nest in the picturesque mill house, which has two millstones propped up by the gate, and others have been used in crazy paving for garden decoration nearby.

The outing can end at West Keal church, perched on the very last, steep edge of the Wolds, the same height as Boston Stump, which is visible to the south across miles of reclaimed Fens. West Keal church, notable for carvings in the porch and nave, has a tall wooden staircase which rears up almost like a ladder. Some of the buttresses of local green sandstone have had to be repaired with bricks because of weathering and the attacks of a stone-boring insect, the mason bee, which has chewed holes up to three inches deep.

Tennyson Country

Sooner or later most visitors to the Wolds will go to Somersby,

Tennyson's birthplace. On the way there from Spilsby is an area where Dr Samuel Johnson comes on the scene. He had Lincolnshire friends in the captivating southern part of the Wolds. Partney, for instance, was the home of Peregrine Langton, whose nephew Bennet, of Langton by Partney, was a friend of Dr Johnson's and brought him over on a visit. Peregrine Langton's 'art of life' interested Johnson so much that he advised the nephew, without success, to write an account of how the old man lived so well on so little—£200 a year.

Dr Johnson came to visit Bennet Langton on several occasions, though Langton Hall, where he stayed, has gone, and its successor too has been demolished. In 1800 Bennet's son, another Peregrine, married a Massingberd heiress and took that family name. Down by the stream which flows into the Lymn is a delightful little round rustic cottage with a steep thatched pyramid of a roof. Langton church stands a short distance up the road, an early eighteenth-century building with an octagonal bell turret. The interior would have delighted Thomas Hardy. As at Well, the pews face sideways, there is a three-decker pulpit under a sounding board, and a gallery, though the Langton gallery is smaller and lighter, and the Langton ceiling is plainer.

From Langton by Partney you can make your way by lanes with wide grass verges or grassy banks, some supporting oaks, to Harrington. The medieval church, with an odd-looking chimney pot, was practically rebuilt in Victorian times but still extant are monuments to families who lived in the Hall. A cross-legged knight may represent Sir John Harrington, who died around 1300. Other monuments are to the Copledyke family, whose name is spelled in several ways—Copuldyk, Copledike and Copeldyck. There is no mistaking Charles Amcotts's name. His ancestor, Vincent Amcotts, rebuilt the Hall in 1673, leaving part of the long Elizabethan front and the elaborate porch. Tennyson's father knew the contemporary Amcotts and memories of the lovely walled and terraced garden may have inspired Alfred when he wrote 'Come into the garden, Maud'.

In the vicinity of Harrington, at Smack Dam corner, a plantation of conifers makes a suitable fairytale background for the old-world garden of an enchanting little cottage, its thatch carefully renovated

11. West front of Lincoln cathedral, 'out and out the most precious piece of architecture in the British Isles' (John Ruskin)

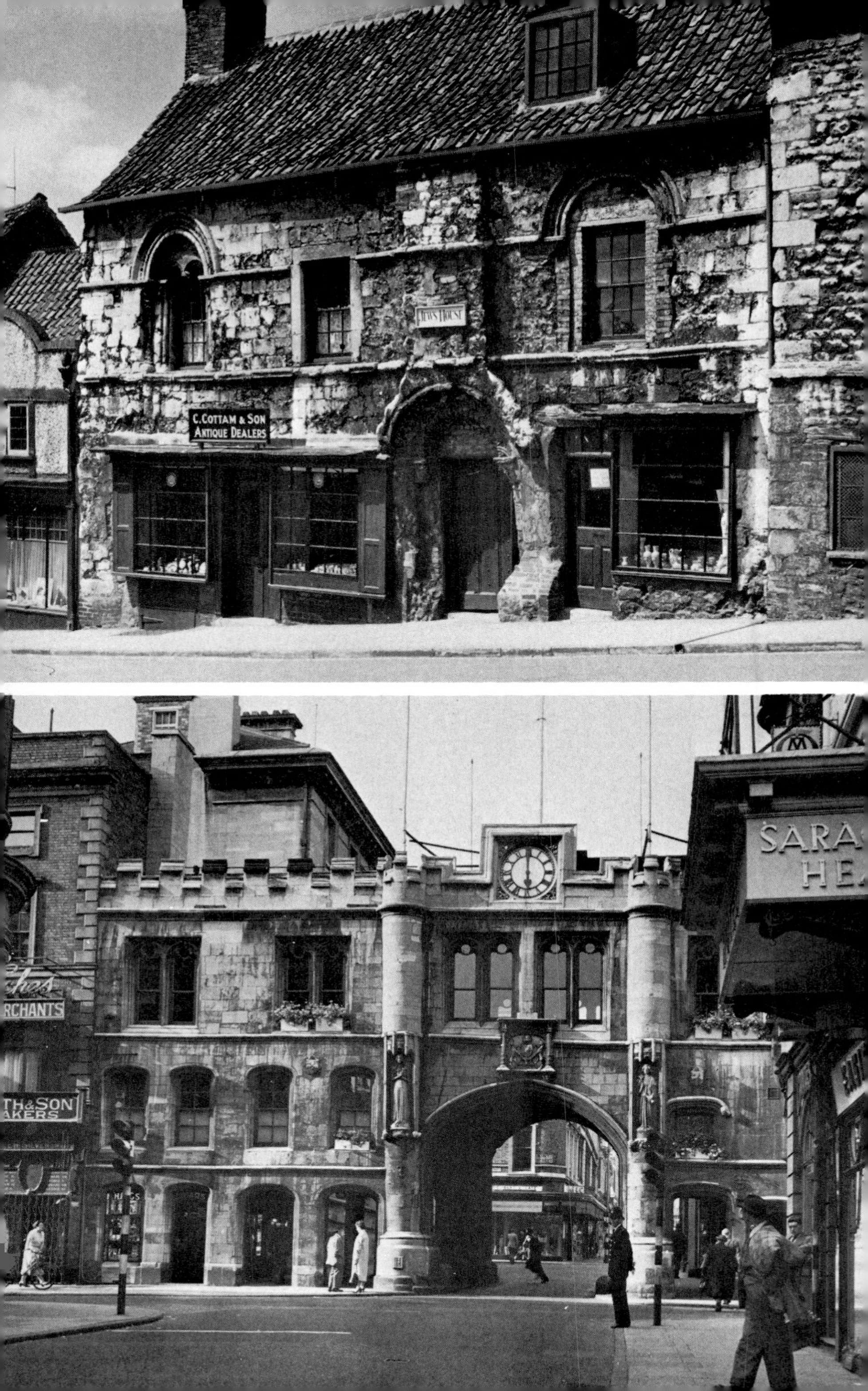

JEWS HOUSE
C. COTTAM & SON
ANTIQUE DEALERS

under the chimney stacks and their brick diamond pattern. The cottage is on the way to Bag Enderby, where Wesley is said to have preached in the open air. In the hamlet's name, the Bag has the significance of 'sac' in cul-de-sac, which is not a bad description of its situation. Some years ago the church had a plague of mice which attacked the organ and chewed up the white notes but left the black ones. Tennyson's father was rector of Bag Enderby as well as Somersby.

The Tennysons came from Yorkshire and are first known in Lincolnshire about 1700 at Barton and at Wrawby near Brigg. Dr George Clayton Tennyson arrived in Somersby in 1808. The rectory is now Somersby House, privately owned and not open to the public. Adjacent is Manor Farm, which may have been designed by Sir John Vanbrugh and is said to be Mariana's moated grange. It was years after the poet's death that a memorial, a bust, was put up to him in Somersby church. The fact is that the Tennyson association with Somersby was not entirely happyy. Dr Tennyson's moodiness, or worse, darkened the years of his incumbency, at least one son was addicted to opium, and the family left after a business failure. That was in 1837, six years after Dr Tennyson's death. Of course Alfred Tennyson did know happiness there as a child and afterwards, especially in the years of his friendship with Arthur Hallam, whom he had met at Cambridge. It was Hallam's death (by drowning) which inspired *In Memoriam,* the turning point in Tennyson's fortunes.

Of late, interest in Tennyson's verse has revived among critics —the poetry-reading public has never neglected his melody and haunting beauty of phrase. The critics have come to admire the sardonic, disturbing note in poems from 'The Vision of Sin' onwards. Tennyson's dialect poems, 'The Northern Farmer' being the best known, are fortunately available in very effective modern recordings, so the toughness of mind and the psychological insight in them is more widely appreciated than ever. Tennyson's own voice, reciting 'The Charge of the Light Brigade', has often been broadcast from an early recording. The Tennyson Society holds a commemoration service each year at Somersby or a neighbouring church around the date of the poet's birthday on 6th August.

12 & 13. Medieval Lincoln: the twelfth-century Jew's House on Steep Hill and the Arch of the Stonebow (fifteenth-century), spanning the High Street

The bells of Hagworthingham church are said to have been the wild ones that Tennyson ordered to ring out, but they have been silent since 1972, when the church tower suddenly collapsed only hours after a flower and harvest festival had ended. It had been known that the massive brick tower needed repairs but the 240 parishioners had not the means to restore it completely, and sadly now it is only possible to make the edifice safe, perhaps at the cost of selling the bells, which are still there, as is the weathercock.

More of the picturesque lanes lead back into the heart of the Wolds, bringing us to the woods around South Ormsby. In the church, as well as wild-haired figures round the font (as at some Marsh churches), there are brasses to the Skipwith family, who took over from the de Ormsby family to whom the Conqueror granted land here. In turn the Skipwiths were succeeded by the Massingberds, who came from the fen country. Drayner Massingberd, a Parliamentarian, is said to have done away with a village on his estate to make room for sheep, on which his fortune was based, permitting him to lay out the garden and stock his lake with fish —not the trout for which it is envied today. James Paine rebuilt South Ormsby Hall in 1752, though the top (third) storey was removed in the 1930s. The Great Eau rises at Campaign Farm a mile up from the Hall and runs into the pretty lake, helping to discourage weed.

From South Ormsby we can go across to Tetford, a charming village with a greenstone church containing a memorial to honour the Champion, Edward Dymoke. The White Hart Inn at Tetford had a Gentlemen's Literary Club, visited by Dr Johnson when he came to stay with Bennet Langton, and later by Tennyson. The Roman road from Burgh le Marsh passes through Tetford and carries straight on towards Nab Hill, while the modern road swerves off to run at the wall of the Wolds. As the modern road climbs Tetford Hill, an older road it has replaced runs alongside at a higher level. This section is a great place for flowers of the chalk.

We have now joined the finest road in Lincolnshire, the Blue Stone Heath Road, which goes for over twelve splendid miles without a house. The Blue Stone Heath Road is said to follow an ancient trackway. On its way north it keeps to crests of the Wolds, the land falling away on each side, presenting some magnificent views. The road has the wide verges characteristic of Wolds highways, in parts thick with cow parsley, from which as a boy I used to fashion pea-shooters. In those days an old woman tried to persuade me that blackberries (which also abound) are not fit to eat after Michaelmas Eve, because then the Devil goes round and spits on them. After some hesitation, I disproved the theory by experiments. Certain stretches of the Blue Stone Heath Road are being planted with trees, an innovation regarded at present as controversial, since they will alter the character of the road.

At the top of Tetford Hill a by-road leads to Belchford, almost shut in by hills, in a valley often described as the loveliest we have. It must dispute the claim of others, for instance the one which holds the beauty spots of Oxcombe, Farford and Maidenwell. The Corporation of Basingstoke owns Maidenwell, which has a connection with Bonnie Prince Charlie. In 1744, after landing at Saltfleet, the prince stayed some weeks at Maidenwell. During his visit he insisted on attending a masked ball in Lincoln, where he thought to remain unrecognised by declining to remove his mask at the appointed time, thereby of course calling attention to himself, jeopardising his life, his friends and his future. His identity is said to have been guessed but nobody betrayed him. At one time Maidenwell was given a wide berth by the faint-hearted, for there was no knowing when a ghostly coach and horses might appear, driven by a coachman whose head rested on the box beside him.

The Northern Wolds

A good introduction to the northern part of the Wolds is to set off along the small roads from Louth to Caistor, a journey through characteristic upland country of wide views across fields and ridges, necessitating more use of gears than is customary in Lincolnshire.

Over Limber Hill is Binbrook, a favourite among Wold villages. It has an open square, once a market centre, and old houses and odd corners. Much business was done at the cross in the churchyard from as far back as the thirteenth century. Binbrook has become well known in our days as an RAF station for Bomber Command during the last war, when the Royal Australian Air Force was there, and more recently for Fighter Command. The village gave its name to a township in Ontario, Canada, in the County of Wentworth, adjoining the County of Lincoln, which is no doubt best known for the Niagara Falls.

During the nineteenth century Binbrook was one of the places where gangs of women and children were recruited for exhausting work in the fields under conditions so brutalising that public outcry led to the abolition of the practice. Slightly later, Binbrook was also involved in the drive to organise farmworkers into trade unions, beginning about 1872 with the activities of William Banks of Boston and Joseph Arch from outside the county.

The winding roads do not go through many villages, though there are several off on either side, and you may find time to search them out in the hollows of the Wolds. Soon, on the left, for instance, the longest stretch of unfenced road in Lincolnshire runs to a prettily situated hamlet, Stainton le Vale, with trees round a small lake feeding a stream which in time and after joining others becomes the Tetney Drain. During a particularly severe winter, people in Louth became worried about the plight of Stainton's isolated inhabitants, but they need not have been afraid, since the driver of the local snowplough lived there and he took his plough home every night, so they were not cut off. Stainton used to be one of the villages known for mumping. The mumpers were women who went round inviting gifts—no shame was attached—and received goods in kind. The day of this custom varied but at Stainton it was St Thomas's Day, 21 December.

Going on towards Rothwell, the small roads encourage no more than an amble, so there is a good chance to enjoy the landscape. Whatever the season, there is always something to look at. In high summer it may be the harvesting of a field of mustard, which is grown only on contract; a tricky crop, but if it comes off, very profitable. Nor does it demand a vast acreage. A man with thirty acres or so is to be envied—that is, if it succeeds. To the untrained eye there is not much difference between a field of mustard and one of charlock, which is still growing in September, to be ploughed in as green manure. Here on the Wolds they will be burning the stubble in September, about a month later than on the lowland arable, the fires patterning the fields with immense charred stripes. In another place there may be what looks like a Forestry Commission plantation of young conifers, but they will be a field of bolted mangolds.

And so after one or two gradients which are steep for Lincolnshire (one in eight, for instance; warning sign duly provided), we come to Caistor, which seems to be losing its grip on the slope of the Wolds and to be sliding down into the valley of the Ancholme. An unusual number of roads converge on Caistor, a pleasant small town centred on its market square surrounded by brick houses built before nineteenth-century taste was blighted, and with a Sessions House over the Butter Market.

Caistor has a long history before the Norman Conquest. According to Camden, Britons had a settlement here called Caer Egarry, and the Romans founded a station, as can be seen from parts of the walls still remaining. Both peoples may have been attracted by a copious water supply from springs where the chalk meets boulder clay, but the water has caused subsidence which has left few traces of the eight acres or so covered by the Roman town. Saxons followed the Romans and modified the name to Tunna Ceaster, or Thong Caster, usually taken to indicate that the site was on a tongue of the Wolds. When the Normans came, Earl Morcar held the district but the Conqueror gave the church to Bishop Remigius to help pay for Lincoln cathedral. In the church are memorials to three knights, two of them de Hundons, and a curiosity, a gad whip which was cracked and flourished on Palm Sunday by a man from Raventhorpe near Broughton, where land was held. It seems that long ago a boy was beaten to death by a branch of wicken (wych elm) for trespassing on Hundon Hills, and an eye-witness of the ceremony said in 1931 that this is the reason for 'the bit o' wicken tree bound round the whip stock'. Caistor Grammar School goes back in part to 1631 and part of the Roman wall is built into it. The poet Sir Henry Newbolt, who wrote 'Play up and play the game', was a pupil.

One of the roads north from Caistor meets woods which stretch for six miles. Where pylons march across a northern shoulder of the

High Wolds there is a square, tapering tower, Pelham's Pillar, built in 1849 for Charles Anderson Pelham. On the Pillar you can read why it was put up—to celebrate the planting of trees by the first Baron Yarborough. The planting is among the most enterprising feats undertaken in Lincolnshire. In 1787 Lord Yarborough started to reafforest his estate on a gigantic scale. By 1823 he had planted 12,552,700 trees. His descendants have continued the work on an even bigger scale. When the fourth Earl of Yarborough died in 1936 more than thirty million trees had been planted, nearly half that total by him. Native species predominate but there are also exotics. Maintenance and management of the woods are conducted according to modern techniques of forestry.

A thousand-acre park surrounds Brocklesby, seat of the Earls of Yarborough, now in the extreme north of the county. At the Great Limber end of the park is a clump of cedars and a mound, where Roman remains have been discovered, and on the mound is the greatest monument of Brocklesby, the circular neo-classical Mausoleum. It was designed by the architect James Wyatt as a memorial for Sophia Aufrere, who died in 1787, the wife of the first Lord Yarborough. Inside, a pedestal bearing a statue of Sophia by Joseph Nollekens rises from a floor patterned with marble and brass. Three recesses hold monuments to other Pelhams (the family name of the Earls of Yarborough).

During Wyatt's stay at Brocklesby he also designed the dog kennels—the Brocklesby Hunt is famous beyond Lincolnshire—and the conservatory has been attributed to him, as has the Holgate Monument, put up by the first Baron to the memory of George Holgate, a farmer, 'a tenant and friend', according to the inscription.

It is not known who designed the grotto and the root house, where rustic furniture is set among the branches of the trees, and the memorial arch over a drive west of the Hall. Nor is it known what, if anything, Humphry Repton did at Brocklesby, beyond mentioning the lake in his *Sketches* of 1794. But it is known that Capability Brown worked at landscaping the park, and that he was responsible for the East Hall of the house in 1772, with 'a great deal of trouble', and he has been given credit for the seven-arched bridge and also a temple to Arabella Aufrere. A Lincolnshire architect working in London, Charles H. Tatham, added the single-storey picture gallery in 1807, and perhaps the orangery, which contains antique sculpture brought from Appledurcombe House on the Isle of Wight.

Brocklesby Hall, or more properly, Park, was built for William Pelham in 1603 but it was rebuilt of brick a good century later, reputedly on the model of Buckingham House. Since then there have been several reconstructions, the most recent making it smaller and more like the early eighteenth-century building. Wallis of Louth did some of the wood carving in the house.

The lead broach spire of Brocklesby church rises above the wooded park. The organ, a handsome instrument dated 1773, was brought from the great house. There are monuments in alabaster and marble to Pelham ancestors in the church, some bearing the peacock symbol of the Pelhams and some the buckle which was the family badge, granted to Sir John Pelham for having captured King John of France at Poitiers in 1356.

THREE

Ancholme and Trent

The Ancholme Valley

In 1793 a canal was cut to link Caistor to the Ancholme but the waterway stopped short of the town and is now disused. The Ancholme itself has been canalised, apparently by a man with a ruler, judging by its almost painfully straight course, so unlike the loopings of the old river, which have been permitted to exist. In our day, as in Drayton's, the Ancholme is famous for 'fat and dainty eels'.

The valley is a great farming area. Poultry are reared on a large scale. Peas cover hundreds of acres for quick freezing or canning. Quantities of cereals are grown for seeds, new species being developed and tested before distribution. Though crops are in general taking over from stock, there are still numbers of cattle, sheep and pigs on the farms.

This agricultural scene is overlooked from the upland villages along the western edge of the Wolds. A typical one is Bigby, its church holding a very unusual nine-sided font and monuments to the Tyrwhit family. Crouching over the alabaster figure of Sir Robert Tyrwhit (died 1581) is a hairy Wodewose, apparently tugging at the mat on which Sir Robert lies, perhaps trying to get a share of it for the wife and 22 children. A slightly later Sir Robert Tyrwhit also lies in Bigby, the one who induced a maid of honour to Elizabeth I to run away and marry him, to the queen's great displeasure. The errant maid, Lady Bridget Manners, has lost her head from the monument. The Tyrwhits feuded with the Ross family of Melton Ross, and

James I ordered the Melton gallows to be set up by the roadside as a hint that the families should keep the peace.

In the Ancholme valley the villages have their 'Carrs', low-lying peaty stretches which they reclaimed. The carrs are found northwards into Humberside and westwards beyond the Trent into Axholme and Nottinghamshire.

To the west, under the limestone ridge, is one of the best Georgian houses in Lincolnshire—Norton Place, built by John Carr in 1776 for John Harrison. The park has been planted with trees set about a narrow lake crossed by a bridge. Norton Place is near Glentham, and Glentham church has a stone effigy of a lady, perhaps of the Tournay family from Caenby on Ermine Street, but for long known as Molly Grime. Seven old maids used to be paid a shilling each on Good Friday for washing this figure. 'Molly Grime' is said to be a corruption of Maelgren, signifying holy image washing, and the custom (discontinued in 1832) is regarded by some as a survival of washing the effigy of the dead Christ. Someone told Miss Rudkin, author of *Lincolnshire Folklore,* that a man called Newell left money to seven poor widows of Glentham on condition that they fetched water from a well some distance west of the village to wash 'a stone coffin-top'; and since the custom had been given up 'these many years . . . I often wonder *what's become of the money?*'

Out among the lowland farms are villages rarely visited except by those who know of their churches. Buslingthorpe, for instance, has one of the oldest brasses in the country. Discovered in 1707, it is the half figure of Sir Richard Buslingthorpe, wearing chain mail, with a heart between his hands, which are protected with gloves plated like an armadillo. The brass was formerly dated about 1290 but the early fourteenth century is now considered more likely. Another knight, cross-legged, in mail armour, may be an effigy of Sir John de Buslingthorpe from late in the thirteenth century. He has been rescued from the indignity of serving as a paving stone in the floor by the pulpit, where he must have lain face down for hundreds of years. Fortunately he looks little the worse for his experience, and in fact it may have protected him.

In 1915 Cox considered Snarford 'a small village with a small church . . . which is of no architectural importance . . . But the fabric is of some celebrity for giving shelter to some remarkable monuments of the St Paul family, which some folk style 'magnificent' and others 'beautiful'; to our mind they are strange and unpleasing, though doubtless splendid of their style. When visited ... they were undergoing restoration'. Now the monuments are restored, and the impression they make on you can be compared—or contrasted—with Cox's opinion. It will be surprising if you find them 'unpleasing'. In the chancel the alabaster figures of Sir Thomas St Paul (or St Pol) and his wife lie on their tomb under an alabaster canopy supported by six posts. The great monument, dated 1582, is elaborately ornamented and decorated. Sir Thomas lies on his back in the chapel, Sir George St Paul (1613) rests on his elbow in the wall monument, and so does his wife Frances. The lady reappears, again as wife, on an alabaster tablet for Robert Lord Rich, Earl of Warwick, who died in 1619. The second husband, Rich, was the 'Rich fool' who contrived to marry as his first wife Penelope Devereux, the beloved Stella of Sir Philip Sidney's sonnet sequence in which he is Astrophel. Rich divorced Penelope and ten years later married Frances St Paul. She survived Rich also, dying in 1633.

A tributary of the Ancholme, the Rase, links three places called Rasen. Market Rasen is, of course, widely known because of its National Hunt racecourse. The town is in a grazing district, noted for its sheep, but during Elizabethan times a local crop was woad. The De Aston Grammar School was built a century ago, though it is still partly financed from income from a medieval endowment of Thomas de Aston's, Canon of Lincoln, who set up a hermitage at Spital on Ermine Street. Until last century, Shrove Tuesday in Market Rasen was the occasion of a rampage given the excuse of a football game, in which all and sundry joined. The object was to get the ball into Middle Rasen by fair means and foul. Canny householders along the road would board up their windows.

By common consent the church at Middle Rasen possesses, in its south doorway and chancel arch, some of Lincolnshire's best Norman work. At the third of the Rasens, West Rasen, the river flows through the three arches of a fourteenth-century packhorse bridge. The road, which has just made a right-angle turn, prefers to use a modern bridge.

South of Market Rasen, near Linwood, it is possible to find a brown, rather ferocious-looking little plant, its fronds edged with spines which turn out to be blunt. It is Iceland Moss, or bread moss, a northern species rare in Britain but still eaten by the Lapps when they have no bread. Eating it at Linwood is forbidden and I do not recommend it anywhere, as it contains harmful acids even after being boiled. Despite the word moss in its names, it is a lichen.

The presence of Iceland Moss reveals the lasting influence of the Ice Ages. Glaciers left gravel and sand, especially sand, over boulder clay. One belt of sand stretches from Market Rasen to the Isle of Axholme. Glaciers thus altered the landscape and redistributed soils, hence affecting the vegetation. Once there were extensive heathlands around Market Rasen. A remnant is Linwood Warren, 66 acres of which form the Cornwallis Memorial Reserve, its name commemorating R. K. Cornwallis, co-author with A. E. Smith of *The Birds of Lincolnshire.*

At Linwood we still find, though partly by chance, species of trees which colonised Britain after the ice retreated. There are pines, which have been reintroduced, birches, creeping willow and oak, as well as the lime or linden which gave Linwood its name. There is great variety in a small area, from grassland to bracken, heather and marsh plants, including sundew. The variety makes for a rich wildlife population. Red squirrels still occur, for instance. Given luck, you may hear the croaking of a woodcock at dusk in the breeding season, or the curious guttural trill of a nightjar. You may see an adder, perhaps a slow-worm, certainly many butterflies and even more moths.

Various dams and sluices have been ingeniously devised to maintain the water level in low-lying parts of the reserve. Even the grazing cows and horses are there for a purpose—to control the spread of coarse grasses and rushes. Clearance of birch and Scots pine has to be done by the management team, or the scrub would displace the heather.

Linwood Warren is near the golf course, one of the modern uses of the area. Stone Age man settled and hunted here, and left flint instruments; in Roman times, potters built their kilns; medieval farmers constructed banks to mark their fields. A hundred years ago,

Market Rasen volunteers practised at the butts of a rifle range on the Warren, and during the First World War, infantrymen were trained in practice trenches.

For hundreds of years sheep have more or less safely grazed here. They made the fortune of John Lyndewode, a wool stapler, who died in 1419, and his son, another John, who survived him by only two years. Each has a famous brass under a canopy in Linwood church, the younger John with his feet on a woolpack bearing his merchant's mark. William, another son of the older John, had a distinguished career under the Lancastrians as Bishop of St David's and Lord Privy Seal, and he was associated with the founding of Eton College.

The Trent in Lincolnshire

The river Trent forms only a small section of Lincolnshire's western boundary, roughly from opposite Lincoln to just north of Gainsborough. Lincoln and even Grantham are only a few miles within our county's borders. Between them, Nottinghamshire lunges eastwards across the Trent. Once Lincolnshire claimed an area west of the Trent—the Isle of Axholme—but has now lost it.

Izaak Walton quoted opinions that the Trent is 'so-called from 30 kinds of fishes that are found in it, or for that it receiveth 30 lesser rivers'. He also quoted Michael Drayton's line 'The crystal Trent, for fords and fish renown'd'. The fords have gone, and the ferries too which were once a feature north of Gainsborough. Few would describe the Trent as crystal any longer, though in the 1960s salmon were caught in it above Newark. In the reaches we are concerned with, the Trent is unchancy, liable to flood. In 1943 it brimmed over in eleven places, and in 1947 the banks were breached disastrously at Morton. Since then flood defences have been strengthened. In 1910 the Trent was frozen over at Gainsborough; a repetition seems unlikely, because the river is now warmer by several degrees since power stations were built along its left bank.

Just as the Severn (like other places we can all think of) has its Bore, the Trent has its Aegre. This parcel of tidal waves is likewise spelled Eagre, Hugre and Aegir. Since the Morton flood of 1947, which scoured the river bed, the Aegre is less impressive than it used to be ('it always was', according to a Gainsborough friend). Nevertheless, the times of its occurrence are still given in the Gainsborough papers, and indeed it is noticeable a dozen miles upstream from the town. The name of the Trent phenomenon, by the way, is appropriate in that Aegir was the Norse god of the sea, and it was by way of Humber and Trent that many Danish invaders penetrated the English midlands.

The tide is felt along the Trent as far as it has any connection with Lincolnshire. A mile or two away from the river's entering the county, a Dane gave his name to a village: Kettlethorpe. About five centuries later the local knight was Sir Hugh Swynford, who died in 1372, leaving a young widow, Katherine. We have already mentioned how she became John of Gaunt's wife. By then their son Henry Beaufort, born out of wedlock, was Bishop of Lincoln but not yet a Cardinal. He and his three brothers were later legitimised. Only the battlemented gateway of the Swynford Hall remains, unless you count the moat.

The Trent flows on, broad and slow, through a landscape which is broad and flat. It has dykes, which are banks, like those in Holland, not the drainage channels of the Fens. Drainage ditches there are in abundance still, but it is the river that takes the eye—the river, and the passing barges, the wind moving the reeds, the strange pale radiance (rarely stained by fierce colours) of the dome of the sky.

The river's northwards course is once changed briefly to south at a huge loop just before the pylons march over it and about where the railway used to cross. As it resumes its accustomed direction, the road swerves sympathetically, affording a view of the river's junction with a singular waterway from Lincoln, the Fosse Dyke, constructed by the Romans, the oldest canal still navigable in England. Few walks are more peaceful than the towpath of the Fosse Dyke, which can be followed all the way.

On the bank of the Trent here at Torksey, among mole hills and thistles and grazing cows, stands a gaunt and angular ruin in red brick, its silhouette much pierced by windows. In Elizabethan times this Torksey Castle was occupied by the Jermyn family. Royalists took it from Parliamentarian forces in the Civil War, by which time its days were nearly done. Though old, Torksey Castle was a comparative newcomer. The church was here before it, and so were two priories, now vanished utterly. Torksey was a town by Domesday, and retained its importance during the Middle Ages. Still earlier, in 873, a Danish Viking expedition wintered at Torksey, having reached there by water. The Romans seem to have given the place its start as a port at the junction of the waterways. They developed potteries, as archaeologists have revealed at Little London nearby, beginning a tradition which lasted through medieval times and was briefly revived at the beginning of the nineteenth century by William Billingsley, examples of whose rare Torksey ware are preserved in the Usher Gallery at Lincoln.

St Augustine sent Paulinus as a missionary to the north, and Bede tells of a man who had been baptised by Paulinus at noon-day in the presence of King Edwin of Northumbria, with a great number of people, in the river Trent about AD 625. Torksey claims to have been the scene of this mass baptism, but so does Littleborough, some miles downstream on the left bank.

Like Torksey, Marton was once much bigger than it is today. Again like Torksey, it was sited by the Romans, here where a road of theirs led to one of the fords which Drayton picked out as a feature of the Trent. The Roman road is Till Bridge Lane. There is no mistaking who made it. From Ermine Street, north of Lincoln, it drives for the river, dead straight for nine miles, with never a settlement on it. At Marton it crosses the riverside road and goes on to the ford opposite Littleborough, identified as the Roman Segelocum. That ford was used by Harold and his army on the series of forced marches from victory at Stamford Bridge to defeat at Hastings. It might even have been that William, his conqueror, also crossed the Trent here, coming down to take Lincoln after laying Yorkshire waste. When the river is low, people have seen the actual crossing.

On the way to Gainsborough we pass two fine houses, Gate Burton, with a stone temple in the park, and Knaith Hall. Lord Willoughby of Parham is said to have built Knaith Hall, though others attribute it to Thomas Sutton, born in 1532, the founder of the Charterhouse. The black and white timbering which makes

Knaith unusual in Lincolnshire was added in Victorian times.

Lea has a long village green but has become built up as Gainsborough develops. Cromwell came twice to Lea in 1643. Redcoats Field and Graves Close (another field), as well as Cavendish Bog, tell of his battle against Royalist troops commanded by Charles I's godson, Charles Cavendish, who was slain. Although Cromwell was victorious, he had to retreat from greatly superior forces, and this retreat even more than the victory added to his military reputation. Presently he returned, adequately reinforced, securing not only Gainsborough but practically all Lincolnshire.

Most of the Trent's reeling and writhing has ended at the approach to Gainsborough, and in the town there is the last bridge now in Lincolnshire across the river. Beyond Gainsborough there are no longer even ferries.

Gainsborough

Open country surrounds Gainsborough, and woods come down the slopes north of the town. In the town itself, room has been found for parks and open spaces, the centre has been redeveloped, riverside gardens have been provided and other amenities extended. Such changes, making Gainsborough a better place for its citizens, are coming about because it is officially an Expanding Town. An agreement with the Greater London Council for the transfer of population and industry from London has brought many new firms to Gainsborough.

What Gainsborough expanded from is a settlement of Angles. They had come up the Humber and the Trent in the sixth century, and gave their tribal name, Gainas, to the burgh, or borough (fortified township) which they established. Later, as Viking raids seriously threatened England, Alfred the Great planned a series of defensive outposts against them, including Gainsborough, and there he is said to have married Ealswitha, a princess of the Gainas, in 868. Nevertheless, as we have seen, Danes were able to spend the winter at Torksey in 873. Far more importantly, in 1013 the Danish king, Svein Forkbeard, captured Gainsborough; not that it helped him much personally, for he died mysteriously within a few weeks. On

Svein's death his formidable son, the thin-nosed, lucky, devout Canute went on to add the crown of England to the crowns of Denmark and Norway which he already had, making him the greatest ruler in northern Europe.

Medieval Gainsborough clustered round the parish church. In the Market Place a few remaining fragments indicate the kind of timber-framed buildings which then formed the town. Red brick came in during the seventeenth century and this material is still typical of the town. Agriculture was predominant at this period, as confirmed by autumn and Easter fairs and by marts for 'horses and other cattle, all manner of hemp, linen and sack cloth, and other goods sold by pedlars, all corn and grain, all grocers, mercers, habbardashers, silkmen, confectioners, tinmen, scale makers and wares whatsoever". The quotation is from Sir Nevill Hickman's allocation of different parts of the town to groups of trades in 1637. Right up to the enclosures of 1804 the ancient open fields existed east of Gainsborough, and their names remain: Middle Field (now a housing estate), Sand Field, the Northolme and the Southolme.

One of Gainsborough's main streets is Ropery Row, taking its line and its name from a former ropewalk, one of many trades associated with shipping. Gainsborough began to develop as an inland river port before 1700. The town stood just where it was convenient to tranship goods from sea-going to river craft, and handled cargoes going by Trent between the great port of Hull and the growing industrial towns of Nottinghamshire and Derbyshire.

In 1814 a local boy 'ran fit to break my neck to see the ship that had come up the river with a chimney for a mast'. The ship was the *Caledonian,* operating on the Trent only about two years after the *Comet* had first steamed on the Clyde. Within a year the first steamship to be built at Gainsborough was launched, with the appropriate name of the *Trent,* a wooden paddlesteamer of 12 horse-power intended for service between Thorne and Hull. The builders were Furleys, who have been operating vessels on the Trent since 1770.

Presently, the river trade much diminished, firms went out of business and disaster threatened Gainsborough. The cause was the coming of the railways in 1849. Catastrophe did not overtake the

14 & 15. Classical and Romantic: Vanbrugh's north front (1722) to Grimsthorpe Castle and the north front of Harlaxton Manor (1831) by Anthony Salvin

HOTEL
A1
NEWARK
SLEAFORD
LINCOLN

town, however. Gainsborough has never relied only on the river. Soon after the railway boom, farming began to use more and more machines. Engineering firms were established, adding a new and successful industry.

For many people Gainsborough is the Old Hall. It brings a shock of delight to encounter in the middle of the town this splendid medieval manor house surrounded by lawns and flowering trees, all maintained by the Council. You may care to focus on the black-and-white timbering of façade and gables. If you are a chimney fancier, you go to the back of the west wing and admire the five sets of Elizabethan brick chimneys. Walk round a little farther and there are battlements above the windows, and a polygonal tower, reminding some people of Tattershall Castle. The Old Hall as we know it goes back to the fifteenth century, with important modifications late in the sixteenth century, revealing the change from defensive considerations to a greater emphasis on comfort. Extensive renovations have recently been carried out, largely through the efforts of the Friends of the Old Hall Association, working with local and national bodies. The need for restoration is plain when we consider the long history of the Old Hall.

In 1470 the owner was the second Sir Thomas Burgh. In that year, when the Wars of the Roses were devastating the land, the Lancastrians revenged themselves on Burgh, a Yorkist supporter, destroying his house and plundering his estates. By 1484 the manor had been restored in time to welcome Richard III, the last Yorkist king, on a visit to Gainsborough. Henry VIII too visited the Hall, once in 1509 and again in 1540. Lord Burgh's eldest son was then dead, leaving a widow, Katherine, née Parr. Henry may have met her during his second visit; at all events she became his sixth and last wife. Another Thomas Burgh, a statesman under Elizabeth I, was compelled by extravagance to sell all his Gainsborough property before he died in 1597. The purchaser of the manor was William Hickman of London, knighted by James I. He was responsible for renovating the west wing and its splendid chimneys. The Hickmans lived in the Old Hall until 1720. After Lord Abingdon, to whom the Hall was let, no other titled family lived there.

Many changes came to the Hall from then on. Wesley preached

16. *above* Fifteenth-century façade of the Angel and Royal Inn at Grantham;
17. *below* St Peter's Hill, Stamford

there on several occasions, and his followers and those of Whitfield worshipped there, though for a short time after 1769 William Hornby, of the Gainsborough Bank, used it as a linen factory. In 1790 the Hall became a theatre, and several families lived in it rent free. In 1826 a new proprietor, Henry Bacon, gave the panelling to Sir Charles Anderson, who removed it to Lea Hall. Thirty years later the Hall was used as a Corn Exchange, Mechanics' Institute, News Room and Concert and Ball Room. Eventually Sir H. B. Bacon, succeeding to the title and estates in 1872, began the series of restorations of the Hall.

Inside, the wonders of the place are the Great Hall and the medieval kitchens. Massive beams arch from the walls of the Great Hall to support the open roof and the pantiles above. In the kitchen there is an enormous fireplace at each end, and great brick ovens. During sixteen weeks of the grim winter of 1816-17, soup, biscuits, coal, herrings and potatoes were distributed to 435 families from these kitchens. A museum has been built up in the Old Hall.

Gainsborough was a Puritan centre and there was a belief, now discredited, that the Old Hall was used as a meeting place by a group set up about 1602 which was a direct forebear of the Pilgrim Fathers. William Hickman, and even more his mother, Rose, had Puritan sympathies, though he was a conforming Puritan who hoped to influence the church from within. The group, on the other hand, were Separatists, some of those who broke away from the Church of England. Of the group, John Robinson has been claimed as Gainsborough-born, and a John Robinson Memorial Church was built in the town for the Congregationalists in 1896. It is now held more likely that Robinson was born at Sturton le Steeple in Nottinghamshire. There too John Smyth was born, a few years earlier. Smyth was pastor of the Gainsborough Separatists, who also included William Brewster, of Scrooby (Nottinghamshire) and William Bradford, of Austerfield (Yorkshire).

In 1606 the members from west of the Trent broke away from the Gainsborough church and began meeting at Brewster's Scrooby home, with John Robinson as teacher. In 1608 John Smyth led the Gainsborough church to Holland to join other English Separatists. The Scrooby church tried to go too but were betrayed and their leaders imprisoned in Boston. Some months later, women and children of the group travelled by boat from Gainsborough to Immingham, their menfolk going overland, and the whole party managed to get away. It was not long before differences of doctrine and personality led the Scrooby contingent to transfer to Leyden, their pastor being John Robinson. From Leyden the Pilgrim Fathers sailed to Southampton and then in 1620 to America to found the New Plymouth colony. John Robinson stayed in Leyden. There were no Lincolnshire people among the Pilgrim Fathers.

South of the Old Hall, Bridge Street runs parallel to the Trent but separated from it by massive warehouses and commercial buildings which front the wharfage along the river. In 1791 a toll bridge was built (widened in 1964). Iron gates from its early days are now in the new Whitton Riverside Gardens. If you cross the bridge, you can stand by the Trent Port Hotel and look at a painting on its walls of the view of Gainsborough as it was about 1860, the time of George Eliot's novel *The Mill on the Floss.* You look in vain across to the Gainsborough bank for Ashcroft Mill by the bridge, said to be the model, for it has been demolished. Other people claim that Union (or Mercer's) Mill, also by the bridge, also vanished, was what George Eliot had in mind.

The river front is still a fine sight. Old warehouses rear up from sturdy quays, handling cargoes for the flour mills, including maize direct from Rotterdam. The wooden sailing ships and the paddle steamers which replaced them have gone, of course, but there are great barges and modern diesel vessels on the river. Another sight that has gone is the series of windmills on the rising ground behind the town, both post and tower mills. When steam came in, the mills were sited by the Trent. In those days, seed-crushing was one of the chief industries. Linseed was imported, mainly from the Baltic, and linseed oil was exported, the by-product cattlecake finding local markets. One eighth of all the linseed brought to Britain was processed at Gainsborough, though business ceased in 1942.

Nineteenth-century prosperity and growth resulted in a number of new streets being laid out in grid pattern. Many old warrens of dwellings and household industry remained. In one of them, Sailor's Alley, a yard off Bridge Street, Thomas Miller lived, in his day 'the most prolific, the most versatile and the most popular of the writers born in Gainsborough'. The quotation is from a booklet by the Gainsborough Librarian, J. S. English, who rightly says that Miller should be remembered and honoured in his native town. The booklet makes an excellent introduction. During his lifetime from 1807 to 1874 Miller wrote sixty books, including poetry, novels, children's stories and verse, books of nature and country life (still with their appeal) and *Our Old Town,* 1857, of great local interest.

As a boy, Miller was friendly with a neighbour's child, the extraordinary Thomas Cooper, later known as 'the Chartist'. Both boys were reared fatherless, in poverty. Cooper's mother set up as a dyer and also made cardboard boxes, which she carried round the district stacked up on her head. Thomas Cooper was precocious. At three, he taught a seven-year-old the alphabet. Radical brushmakers in Gainsborough lent him their newspapers and when he was sixteen he helped to found and run an Adult School on Sundays to teach labourers to read. He worked at home as a shoemaker, rising at four in winter, three in summer, to study. From seven to lunch he worked, then studied again for half an hour, and worked on until eight or nine at night. He then read until midnight.

In 1828 Cooper opened a school of his own and worked actively for the Wesleyans, but in 1833 he left Gainsborough for Lincoln. He married, became a journalist, later a political agitator in Leicester, was imprisoned at Stafford, turned Baptist evangelist and received two Civil List grants, thanks to the Chartist Holyoake, who declined one for himself and recommended Cooper to Gladstone. Cooper lectured and travelled until he was 80. The Thomas Cooper Memorial Church in Lincoln was erected in 1884, six years before his death.

In the Middle Ages, Gainsborough provided a master mason for Lincoln, and a bishop of Worcester. Of the many other divines from the town, Rev. James B. Mozley, Professor of Divinity at Oxford, would be the most celebrated if it was widely realised that he inspired the character of the Dormouse in *Alice in Wonderland.* The founder of modern geography, as Sir Halford J. Mackinder has been called, was from Gainsborough, and so was Sir Charles Denzil Jeff Ibbetson, the distinguished member of the Indian Civil Service.

FOUR

Under the Cliff

The valleys of the Trent and Witham form a continuous lowland area in western Lincolnshire as far south as Grantham. This lowland is bounded by the long, long sill of rock, the Cliff, and below Lincoln, its continuation, the Edge (of the Heath). Villages in the valley have their portion of high ground, called Cliffs, while villages below the crest of the sill have their Low Fields down in the valley.

North of Gainsborough, turning away from the Trent towards the Cliff, it is a surprise in that generally flat country to find a hill after about a mile. In this setting Hardwick Hill looks far higher than its 130 feet. The Romans had a pottery there and perhaps an iron foundry. From Hardwick Hill you can look out over Scotton Common, where the Forestry Commission has been at work. Disregarding the plantations, it is possible to gain a very fair idea of what so much of England used to be like, namely waste, meaning uncultivated. Parts of it are boggy, the rest has heather, scrub and woodland. Left unchecked, the birch scrub would take over the open heath but the birch is now subject to control. Some forty acres of Scotton Common belong to the Linconshire Trust, which is responsible for managing this nature reserve.

Until our day the acid soil was considered unfit for agriculture. Wildlife could flourish undisturbed. Since afforestation and new farming methods have come in, fewer bird species nest at Scotton. Stone curlews, dunlins, wheatears, whinchats and stonechats are among the losses. Clubmoss and a sundew have also disappeared. Since myxamatosis, rabbits no longer keep down heather and coarse grass. As one result, the grayling butterfly disappeared from Scotton. This was countered in 1972 by the Trust, who reintroduced the butterfly. The Trust also found that the shrubby bog myrtle was threatened elsewhere on the Common, so they established it in the reserve. Under their care many creatures have been able to survive, from the tree pipit to harvest mice, common lizards and adders.

The river Eau (not Great, like the stream on the other side of the Wolds) skirts the Common on its way to the Trent. It flows by Scotton village. The church here is one of those which used to be mentioned as having suffered at the hands of 'that Goth, Archdeacon Bayley', who about 1820 'despoiled every church he could plunder to enrich his own' at Messingham. The indignation is Cox's. The old village stocks are now in the church, perhaps to deter latter-day Goths, though current opinion is noticeably less hostile to Bayley.

From Scotton it is no distance to the crest of the limestone ridge. Along it is the Roman road called Ermine Street. It is as straight as Till Bridge Lane but far longer. Properly speaking, Ermine Street connected London to Lincoln, once the Romans' northern outpost; only later was the road prolonged to the Humber. The name has nothing to do with a stoat's winter fur. Sometimes it is spelled Irmine, and that too hides its derivation from the name of the Anglo-Saxon tribe of Earningas, through whose territory it passed. In the 'Laws of William I' Ermine Street was one of the four roads subject to a special peace. Later in Norman times, those coming south along the Humber extension were the first of all the subsequent travellers who see Lincoln cathedral pale in the distance. North of Lincoln the county has no place of any size on Ermine Street, which before the First World War went through what was described as 'absolutely tenantless country'.

I like Ermine Street but I like another road better, roughly parallel to it and west of it, along the scarp. The alternative road seems more attractive in every way except that it has no name, only the designation B1398. Again there are few villages. It overlooks charming rural scenes for almost its entire length to within a mile or two of Lincoln.

One of the few villages on it is Willoughton, which has been a settlement from prehistoric times, through Roman and old English occupation. The Templars were here, and so was a priory dependent on Angers, but the only traces of them are some depressions. Much later, about 1830, Willoughton had a woman parish clerk. Part of her duties was to make public announcements, aided by a loud-hailer known as a vamping horn. Some villages rang a bell to mark the hours of work in the fields but Willoughton used its vamping horn. The curious instrument, still in the church, is one of very few to survive.

Beyond Glentworth, where they have taken to growing tulips and other spring bulbs as though they were in the Fens, is Harpswell, with its church clock which replaced one presented in 1746 to celebrate the victory at Culloden. Harpswell was the seat of the Whichcot family; their Hall has vanished. About 1700 a Whichcot engaged in a feud with Sir Cecil Wray of Fillingham. Wray had built Fillingham Castle and laid out a park around it, cutting off a right of way dear to Whichcot. Each year Whichcot took his coach and some labourers, pulled down the wall so that he could drive through, crossed the park and returned home. Sir Cecil Wray rebuilt the wall each year. Only Whichcot's death ended this curious tussle of wills.

The afternoon sun brings out the best in Fillingham Castle, a handsome Gothic building with corner towers and battlements, beautifully situated on the hillside. The last time I saw it, a peacock walked across the lawn and flew up on to a window sill. It did not scream and so aroused no memories of the ghost which haunts the corridors of Fillingham Castle, that of a man who committed suicide after an unhappy love affair. Perhaps he is also the shade of a man who has been seen riding a big white horse through the park. Springs in the park give rise to the river Ancholme, which thus finds itself on the wrong side of the Cliff. It promptly disappears from sight, finds a way under the ridge and emerges again a mile or two away, beyond Ermine Street, at the hamlet of Sprindlington.

Fillingham village, below the Castle, is an endearing place. Being near the Cliff, it could use stone for its cottages and the more recent houses. The gardens are well kept and colourful. There are trees on each of the many corners, and others beside. Limes form an avenue to the church. In 1361 the master of Balliol College, Oxford resigned and became rector of Fillingham, where he stayed seven years and gained international fame. He was John Wyclif. While at Fillingham he became openly a heretic, denouncing Papal tribute and proclaiming doctrines which were incorporated into Protestantism.

There is much more of interest farther along the road, but many people will turn aside, here at Fillingham, and make by straight but pleasant lanes westwards for the valley of the Till. The river rises within a short distance of the Trent but does not become a tributary. Among the water meadows, stone is lacking, and brick is used for the flat-topped cottages which seem to be characteristic of the valley hereabouts. On a sunny day the frequent rows of poplars are decorative, but it is easy to imagine their value as windbreaks in stormy weather.

Soon a touchingly haphazard little collection of houses is dwarfed by a massive Romanesque church, that of St Mary's, Stow, called the Mother-Church to Lincoln. The title goes back to before Lincoln cathedral was built. St Mary's, Stow was founded in Saxon times. That much is plain from the great Saxon arches of the crossing, which dominate the interior by their power and strength. No other surviving cruciform church from pre-Conquest times has arches as tall and wide. A glance round the crossing reveals a staircase which, though much worn, leads nowhere. Its age and purpose are unknown, like so much about the development of this great church.

Traditionally the earliest church on the site was built by the Northumbrian king Egfrid in AD 678. When the diocese of Lindsey was separated from Northumbria, this church became the cathedral but was burned by the Danes in 870. Behind the organ, near a Saxon door, a piece of what looks like cinder can be seen, and there are other fire marks in the church, but they may not have been caused by Danish attack. In the following century the bishops moved away to Dorchester on Thames. The bishopric returned to Lindsey soon after 1072, when William the Conqueror appointed Remigius the first bishop of Lincoln. Remigius founded Lincoln cathedral almost at once and also decided to renovate Stow. A church therefore existed and previous repair work is dated shortly before the year 1000, but how old that fabric was is not known. The greater part of St Mary's is from the eleventh and twelfth centuries, Remigius being credited with the present nave, and Bishop Alexander (1123-1148), called the Magnificent, with the rebuilding of the arcaded and vaulted chancel. The north transept (where the cinder is) came to be known as the Becket chapel from the wall painting showing St Thomas à Becket, murdered in December 1178. Only part of the fresco remains but enough to show that it dates from quite soon after Becket's death.

Early in the fourteenth century, piers were built to take the weight of the tower, and the pointed Perpendicular arches were placed so as to be framed by the huge original ones in the crossing. The master craftsman may have been Richard of Stow, who heightened Lincoln cathedral's crossing tower between 1307 and 1311.

Restoration of St Mary's was carried out in the nineteenth century. At the time, relations between the parson and the villagers were bad, and vandalism was committed in the church. Nevertheless a farmer made no charge for blue lias stone dug from his ground for the rebuilding.

The great church at Stow is not the only connection with medieval bishops of Lincoln. Across Till Bridge Lane, where a farm in Stow Park now occupies the site, the bishops had a moated residence. In the Lincoln Treatises of 1186, Giraldus Cambrensis notes that a large and otherwise aggressive swan attached itself to Bishop Hugh (ruled from 1186 to 1200), following him docilely, feeding from his hand and attacking anyone who approached him. It seemed to know when he was coming, for before his arrival it would flap up and down the moat. From the description this bird does not seem to have been a mute swan, the most familiar species in Britain, but an unusually large whooper swan, which is considered too wild to be domesticated.

No proof exists, by the way, that Stow village is the Roman site of Sidnacaster, as has been suggested.

After this détour, we rejoin the B1398 road. Coming up to Lincoln in 1541, Henry VIII is said to have been so pleased by the hospitality at the manor house in North Carlton that he knighted the owner, John Monson. Later the Monson family left the Tudor gables and mullioned windows of North Carlton for South Carlton, then moved to Burton, and nowadays have gone back to live in the Queen Anne manor house at South Carlton. The church at South Carlton has a Monson mausoleum built about eighty years ago in keeping with the family's Tudor and Jacobean associations. Sir John Monson (1625), High Sheriff of Lincolnshire, and his wife have a canopied tomb, with six pillars, the figures recumbent in alabaster, surrounded by eleven children. Two of the sons were falsely accused of being concerned in the murder of Sir Thomas Overbury, but the charges were fortunately disproved. Both had distinguished careers, one as admiral, knighted for gallantry in 1597 after the siege of Cadiz. His son, Viscount Monson, was vindictively hounded by Charles II for being associated with the execution of Charles I.

With an eye for a splendid view, a wealthy Roman built a villa on the slope of the Cliff at Burton. With something of the same eye, centuries later, the park of Burton Hall was laid out not far away. The Hall where the Monsons lived has been largely demolished. As has happened elsewhere, the stables remain. So do almshouses which Sir John Monson founded in the village in 1651.

Lord Monson has leased 82 acres of gravel pits, with some woodland, at Burton to the Lincolnshire Trust for a nature reserve. It sounds as though it would be too near Lincoln for much wildlife but that is not so. Indeed it is one of the most important sites in the county for water birds and wildfowl, some of which winter there and others breed (including great crested grebe). Kingfishers may be seen throughout the year. The Burton Gravel Pits are also frequented by Daubenton, noctule and other bats.

We have reached the Lincoln Gap, not to mention Lincoln itself, but we may as well continue our account of the western districts, because the same pattern of lowland and scarp villages holds for some miles. Lincoln can afford to wait a little, being unique.

One of the finest houses in Lincolnshire, the Elizabethan Doddington Hall, stands in the plain to the west of Lincoln. It was near Doddington that Queen Eleanor died in 1290. The Hall was built some 300 years later. The owner was Thomas Taylor, Recorder to the

Bishop of Lincoln, and the architect is deemed to have been Robert Smithson, whose work included Hardwick Hall and Worksop Manor. Beyond the gabled gatehouse, across gardens and lawns, is the Hall itself, of brick, some dark from overfiring. Three octagonal turrets with lead domes rise above the parapet and the triple chimneys.

Thomas Taylor's son left the estate to his niece, Lady Hussey. She was burdened by the huge fine of £10,000 imposed on her Royalist husband, a descendant of the Lord Hussey executed after the Lincolnshire troubles of 1536. Nearly half was paid in his lifetime and much of the rest by his widow and the widow of his eldest son. In the eighteenth century Sir John Hussey Delaval employed Thomas Lumby, the Lincoln carpenter, to alter the interior. The grand staircase is one of Lumby's masterpieces. Today, as for upwards of a hundred years, Doddington Hall has been the seat of the Jarvis family, whose memorials enrich the church.

A few miles away some short and lowly annals of the poor have been preserved at Eagle by the vicar, Rev. W. D. Shepperd, and published in 1932. Eagle began grandly enough, if we join the minority who believe that it was founded by Egill, son of a Prince of Finland. Under circumstances which escape me, Egill was forced to anticipate William Tell's feat when King Nioung ordered him to split an apple on his wife's head with an arrow. Etymologists are sure that Egill has nothing to do with Eagle, for spelling in old documents includes forms like Acli, suggesting the Saxon word 'ac', our oak. The village was in the wapentake of Graffoe, that is the Grave How or Burial Mound. Stephen gave what he called Eykel to the Knights Templars, who derived much wealth from sheep and wool. We shall have more to say about the Templars presently. After they had been suppressed, oaks from Aycle were sent to repair Somerton Castle in 1312. The Hospitallers, the Knights of St John, took over the Templars's property. Under them the Eagle estate was called the Bailiwick and gave his title to the Bailiff of Eagle, next in rank to the Grand Prior and the Sub-Prior of the Order.

According to an Elizabethan story by Richard Johnson, there was a Red Rose Knight called Tom-a-Lincoln living with a hundred outlaws on Barnsdale Heath near Eagle. When he refused to give up this disreputable life, in spite of his foster-father's pleas, the old man died of a broken heart. The knight sent £100 in atonement to buy a large bell to be rung at Lincoln for the old man's funeral and to be known as Tom-o-Lincoln. It would be appropriate if the bell called Great Tom of Lincoln confirmed the tale; the original Great Tom was recast in 1610, a date which fits in well enough. It was again recast, enlarged, and rehung in the central tower of the cathedral in 1835.

A story goes that plans to sink for coal at Eagle were advanced in the nineteenth century but the coal-owners of Derbyshire bought off the planner, a local worthy named Samuel Russell Collett. In those days the churchwarden, Noah Wass called his residence the Arke, but Collett lived in The Jungle. The Jungle still exists. A vast sweep of magnificently kept lawn leads the eye of the beholder on the road—for The Jungle is still privately owned—towards the densely ivy-hung battlemented façade of what looks like a fortified villa, with one curved corner and one angular. Where the ivy permits a glimpse of the fabric, this is seen to be mostly overburned bricks, many of them fused into huge dark clinkers. There may still be one or two pheasants on the lawns of this remarkable house but the deer, kangaroos and buffalo that were displayed by Collett have long since gone. The present owners have ambitious plans for renovating The Jungle while maintaining its extraordinary front.

South of Eagle, a Roman road draws a firm diagonal across this part of Lincolnshire. It is the Fosse Way, here almost at the end of its length from Exeter, one of the few major Roman roads which did not pass through London. The Lincoln-Newark section carries heavy traffic and it is not, to be honest, an endearing highway. This western part of the country is unusually wooded, thanks largely to the Forestry Commission, which has taken pains to provide controlled access at places and also to set up picnic sites.

Norton Disney, near the Witham, is named after the d'Isigny family, from near Bayeux, who became lords of the manor here in Lincolnshire in the thirteenth century. Walt Disney claimed descent from this family. The direct line ended in 1685, when William Disney was executed after Monmouth's rebellion. The estate was sold to the second Earl of Albemarle, son of General Monk. Later the Clarges family owned it, and later still John Jervis, Lord St Vincent, the admiral, and his descendants.

The Disneys had a castle, and a manor house built from the ruins in 1685, but both have vanished, along with the Roman villa on Potter Hill, excavated in the 1930s. Fortunately we still have the church, once belonging to Sempringham Priory, and its remarkable Disney monuments, three to men, three to women, most of them in a chapel. Explanatory notes are provided on the church wall.

The Disney brass is famous. Its upper part shows William Disney, his wife Margaret Joiner and their nine children. Below them is Richard Disney, with two (successive) wives and twelve children. The names of the seven sons were later cut out to hinder a lawsuit over an inheritance. The first wife was Nele, or Nell, Hussey, grandmother of the executed Lord Hussey. The second was the childless Jane Ayscough, widow of George St Paul of Snarford. Her older sister Anne was martyred for her Protestant beliefs in 1546.

The brass is very late—perhaps about 1580—at least the side we have been considering. Both sides can be seen, and both have been used, which is very unusual. The back turns out to be earlier. It is not English but Dutch, bearing an incomplete account of the endowment of a mass at Walcheren in 1518. Strangely, the rest of the inscription has been found on another brass—also double-sided—at West Lavington in Wiltshire.

Also in the church are St Vincent memorials and two wooden tablets to members of 300 and 301 Polish Squadron, RAF, killed on duty.

In his poem 'The Deserted Village', Oliver Goldsmith calls Auburn the 'loveliest village of the plain'. He was not referring to the Lincolnshire Aubourn near a big bend in the Witham but the description fits well. Aubourn is far from deserted, though its Victorian church is disused. From this church a one-way road system leads to the village, most of it separated by a road with a wide grass verge from the Witham and the old mill. A Domesday fishery here was valued at 1,000 eels a year. Aubourn has another church, also no longer used, a remarkable one, for the earliest known vicar, Geoffrey, was there in 1076. The chancel which still stands at the end of a field path goes back to about 1200, and other surviving parts of the building are medieval. The tower is an exception, being added about 1862. In the church are monuments to the Elizabethan Sir Anthony Meres and to Sir Christopher Nevile (1692) and Mrs Elizabeth Nevile (1745). These two families were associated with Aubourn Hall and greatly altered and extended the Tudor building inside and out.

Near the Witham is the river Brant, smaller but very independent for as long as possible, flowing for some miles through a plain which is empty of villages. At last, above the fields and hedges and copses, a very elegant spire on a tower can be seen long before the village of Brant Broughton is reached, with its long broad street of stone or brick houses. The church has twin porches, both admirable. Two local families helped to beautify the interior of Brant Broughton church in the past century. One was the Coldron family of smiths, who contributed ironwork. The other family, the Suttons, designed and made stained glass. Robert Coldron links up with them because he made wheels for the clocks which were another passion of the Suttons. Two brothers, Augustus and Frederick, were the stained glass enthusiasts. Both were canons of Lincoln cathedral, for which they provided the glass in 43 windows, the work of their own hands, according to a claim on a brass plate in the nave. Bishop Oliver Sutton of Lincoln (1280-1299) was of the ancient family, which came to Brant Broughton in the seventeenth century. Augustus was the clockmaker and he passed on his interest to his son Arthur, a canon too. Together they set about providing clocks for parishes in Lincolnshire and Norfolk unable to afford one. A silver kettle presented to father and son was engraved with the names of 365 parishes they helped in this way, but the list is incomplete. At Stow, where Canon Arthur Sutton made and installed the clock, he was remembered as going dressed in top hat and frock coat from church to church working on his gifts. Before his death in 1925, Brant Broughton rectory contained forty clocks, each striking the quarters, all chiming together.

Brant Broughton has a Meeting House Lane where the Quakers' Meeting House preserves much of the looks and atmosphere it must have had at its foundation in 1761. When Kesteven had an Education Committee, it ran a Youth Service Residential Centre in the Old Vicarage on the outskirts of the village, behind a drain that looks like a moat.

In the hamlet of Stragglethorpe the road takes a sharp turn at a small church, some of it Anglo-Saxon, some Norman, its fittings Georgian. The church faces a dovecote by the drive to the restored Elizabethan Hall. The Hall was once an offshoot of Sempringham Priory, and monks from the Hall are believed to have built the village church. The Earle family owned the Hall after the dissolution of the monasteries and when in 1697 Sir Richard Earle died, aged only 24, the property reverted to his mother's family, the Welbys of Denton. As you go up the drive to the Hall, where there are likely to be peacocks perching on the roof of the stables, you see what is claimed to be the most northerly vineyard in the world. Vines were planted by the present owner, Major Alan Rook, in the walled kitchen garden in 1964. The first vintage was made in 1967 and yielded 50 dozen bottles. Since then the Lincoln Imperial wine has become known to many connoisseurs.

Now from the lowlands we pass to the Heath. On the Grantham road a string of attractive villages have sprung up, each perched on the very edge of the high ground, which falls away precipitately enough in places to resemble a toboggan-run.

The series extends from Harmston, with its long association with the Thorold family, through Coleby, associated with the Listers, the Scropes and the Tempests, to Welbourn, which was the birthplace of Field-Marshal Sir William Robertson, the only marshal to rise from the ranks.

Boothby Graffoe has a nineteenth-century church but is better known because an earlier church was 'extirpated by a hurricane' in 1666, so completely, it seems, that the very record is not here but at Wellingore nearby. A switchback road leads down, across the abandoned railway track, into the valley of the Brant where, among Boothby Graffoe Low Fields, several moats and an earthwork surround the ruined Somerton Castle. It is now privately owned and undergoing restoration. After King John of France had been captured by Sir John Pelham at Poitiers in 1356, the king and his son Philip were brought to Somerton (1359-60) but he was allowed—perhaps encouraged—to provide lavishly for his whole retinue.

The Grantham road widens to the broad main street of Navenby, where car drivers pull up outside the antique shops. The church is partly on the road. The showpiece in the lovely chancel is the Easter Sepulchre which, though small, has been compared with those of Heckington and Lincoln cathedral. Back from the road, Navenby is one of the quaintest of the villages along this stretch, built on a promontory of the ridge almost cut through on the south by a ravine.

The limestone plateau of the Heath takes a step down at Leadenham and the step provides a wonderful site for Leadenham Old Hall, built for the Beresfords, and Leadenham Hall, where later the Reeves lived as lords of the manor. Both families have memorials in the church, the altar being formed of a Beresford table tomb. The ceiling of Leadenham church was decorated by Pugin in 1841. Since the Grantham road is crossed at Leadenham by the road to Sleaford, it was natural that travellers should be catered for, and two Georgian inns were built, both retaining their popularity as friendly places. Only a few yards from the traffic are twisting village streets that still seem like country lanes.

Fulbeck is so pretty (the best of it off the main road) and Caythorpe church has a strangely swollen spire and a double nave, and both villages are interesting as well as attractive, but do not let them detain you too long from going down into the head of the Brant valley.

The Brant has its source in a combe of the uplands overlooked by round-topped Loveden Hill. Here a round barrow built with a flat top did not yield Bronze or Iron Age finds but Saxon burials from pagan times, 32 bodies interred but no less than 1,245 cremations. Excavations have continued recently, and I recall being told by a young man of how he was ploughing behind the wood at the time and saw skeletons unearthed with the feet cut off and laid beside the bodies, one of them a child's.

Some time after the cremations and inhumations on Loveden Hill, the local Saxons were converted to Christianity and built a church in the sort of commanding position dear to the Barrow Folk, at Hough on the Hill. The church tower dates in part from before the Conquest, and the part that does is easily distinguishable, namely the

18 & 19. Lincolnshire country houses: Gunby Hall (1700), Tennyson's 'haunt of ancient peace', and the Jacobean front, modified 1785, of Casewick Hall, near Stamford

BATEMANS
THE
BRITANNIA
GOOD HONEST
ALES

lower storeys. It may be that the staircase turret, which is an unusual feature, was added later. Near the Saxon window incorporated into the porch, someone long ago patterned the stone seats with a design calling to mind solitaire boards, an oblong enclosing lines connecting eight hollows suitable for marbles. It may be fanciful to imagine that monks played here when there was a priory of Austin canons belonging to an abbey at Cherbourg, and downright unlikely that King John was in the mood when he stayed with them before going on to die at Newark.

A mile or two away from Hough on the Hill is the railway, and beyond that the A1, but they leave untouched several villages in this corner of Lincolnshire remaining curiously remote until stock-car racing enthusiasts discovered it. Sometimes dwarfing the cottages and farm buildings are enormous, painfully new corrugated-iron barns.

One of the oldest Lincolnshire families, the Thorolds, has been here at Marston for hundreds of years. They are often said to be of the same family as Lady Godiva. The sheriff of Lincolnshire when the Normans came was a Thorold. Early in the fourteenth century Sir Richard Thorold married an heiress of the de Marston family and acquired Marston Hall, still a Thorold home. The present house is basically a Tudor manor; it suffered much from Roundhead soldiery, for the owner then, Sir William Thorold, was a Royalist, created baronet by Charles I. Marston Hall is frequently opened to the public, who can go through the eighteenth century rooms still occupied by the family and see the still earlier plasterwork and the collection of furniture, portraits and other paintings. The garden is notable for two trees—a wych elm so enormous that it resembles a grove, and a laburnum which at the age of 400 may be the oldest in England. Since 1962 there has been a little Gothick gazebo in the garden. Thorold monuments in Marston church include a handsome one of Sir Anthony (1594), sheriff of Lincolnshire, and Anne Lady Hodgson (1719) who founded almshouses at Ruskington near Sleaford. For several generations a Thorold was rector of Hougham, the next village, and the imposing Georgian rectory (no longer used as such) was built for them.

In the eighteenth century Sir John, the ninth Baronet, decided to

20. Boston Stump, 272 feet high, a masterpiece of Perpendicular

move to Syston, a few miles away, and had a grand house built by a Grantham architect, John Langwith. The tenth Baronet, also Sir John, collected books, and in 1824 a library was added to Syston Hall by Lewis Vulliamy. Sad to say, the Hall has been pulled down. Five hundred acres of park still contain the large rectangular lake and woodland, with some fine individual trees. The Thorolds have gone back to the Old Hall, rebuilt in 1830 but retaining its Jacobean porch beyond the great courtyard. Syston church naturally has its Thorold monuments, that to the fourth Baronet—once more a Sir John (1716)—being outstanding. The 'Willingham' of Scott's *Heart of Midlothian* is sometimes identified as Syston.

FIVE

Lincoln

By this to Lincoln come, upon whose lofty scite
Whilst wistly Witham looks with wonderful delight,
Enamour'd of the state, and beauty of the place,
That her of all the rest especially doth grace . . .
Michael Drayton's *Poly-Olbion*

Lindon, Lindum, Lincoln

Approaching Lincoln from the south, as the road over Bracebridge Heath drops down past the smooth grassland slope of the South Common, the city appears. Crowning it is the noble silhouette of the cathedral, arguably the finest in England, situated in an unsurpassed position on the edge of the precipitous two-hundred foot face of the limestone plateau. Under the bluff, the river Witham flows through the Lincoln Gap. Spilling down from the site of the original settlement on the plateau, the city extends across the river towards South Common.

Objects considered to be votive gifts have been recovered from the Witham, including the Witham iron sword and its bronze scabbard and the bronze Witham Shield, with its spidery boar. Like Stone Age people before them, the lordly warriors for whom these splendid weapons were made did not live in the Witham marshes but up on the bluff. When the Romans paused about AD 47 with the Empire's frontier on the Trent, they founded a military station here called Lindum, a name believed to derive from a British form, Lindon, its syllables associated with pool and hill fort. Lindum was occupied by the Ninth Legion, called Hispana. The camp was later turned into a *colonia,* where former legionaries were granted land. By the third century the Roman town had been extended downhill and was already an inland port by reason of the Fosse Dyke and Carr Dyke.

After the legions were withdrawn about AD 400, a tribe of Angles, the Lindiswaras, took Lincoln. From now on, in general the history of Lincoln followed the course sketched in earlier pages, so here it must suffice to indicate a few developments particularly affecting the city. The influence of the Danes, for instance, cannot be overlooked. They brought prosperity, thanks largely to increased use of the port, they introduced their own system of twelve hereditary lawmen to administer the town, they are remembered by street names such as Danesgate and Clasketgate and, among other legacies, they gave the 'long hundred' of six score, used until our day for marketing eggs.

During the Middle Ages, Lincoln flourished through its command of water-ways by which trade could pass, especially the trade in wool and wool cloth, the famous Lincoln Green and Scarlets. In 1325 Lincoln was made a staple town, so trade in wool from far around had to be transacted there. Fairs and general commerce attracted English merchants and others from as far as Gascony, Lombardy, Hanseatic cities and Denmark.

Disaster came with the Black Death, when half the city's population died between April and August 1349. At this period too, trading abroad was increasingly done in English ships, so overseas merchants attended less frequently. Seaports gained in importance, notably Boston, which became a staple town in 1369. Lincoln lost its monopoly, and trade fell off. With the decline, Lincoln's water-ways were neglected. A further setback resulted from changes in routes, using the bridge across the Trent at Newark, built as far back as 1179, and the new highway, the Great North Road through Grantham, outflanking Lincoln. In the middle of the fifteenth century Lincoln had only a couple of thousand inhabitants, a third of its population at the Conquest. Whereas in the Middle Ages, Lincoln had fifty churches, in 1549 the number of parishes was reduced to thirteen.

Nevertheless, however much reduced, Lincoln survived as a market town. It was the natural centre for a large agricultural area and its trade slowly picked up. The story can be traced in Burton Road, a short walk from Lincoln castle, at an old army barracks dating from about the time of the Indian Mutiny. Nowadays it has another use as the Museum of Lincolnshire Life, displaying objects in everyday use from Elizabethan times to the present day. The material is so varied that many visits are necessary even to look at the vehicles, machines (some working), shop interiors, household items, farm implements, farmhouse gear and the like (and the unlike).

From about the end of the seventeenth century, gentlemen moved into the city, setting up town houses, and social life became richer as a consequence. There was a round of Assembly Room, balls, the theatre, exchange of visits and of course the horse races.

We have already mentioned the gains resulting from eighteenth century developments such as turnpikes, enclosures and the revival of water transport (in which Richard Ellison of Boultham was prominent from 1741, when he leased the Fosse Dyke tolls and improved the canal, making his fortune and adding to Lincoln's prosperity).

We have also stressed the changes brought about by steam power. Lincoln was late in getting a railway line. During the railway boom of 1843 George Hudson, the Railway King, fought hard and unscrupulously to extend his Midland line from Nottingham to Lincoln, in the teeth of unscrupulous opposition from the faction of the London to York line. Hudson won, and in 1846 the first train reached Lincoln. His rivals did not give up; in 1848 the Great Northern brought their line from Peterborough, doubling the inconvenience to Lincoln's High Street by their level crossing. The two crossings were built after an assurance by Canterbury, a pioneer in such matters, that they would not cause even as much inconvenience as turnpike gates in the same situation.

At much the same period, Lincoln was turned into an industrial town by the success of engineering firms. Their rise benefited Lincoln in times of expansion, but during economic crises the dependence of the city on this one industry resulted in unemployment and hardship.

With opportunities for jobs which paid better than farmwork, men and their families left the villages. Lincoln's population in 1801 was 7,000; in 1841 it was nearly 14,000; in 1871 almost 27,000. This influx brought problems of overcrowding and disease (partly because of a bad water supply), which remained serious until well into this century.

'Below hill'

The beauty and dignity of the city on the hill have been contrasted unfavourably with the industrial development 'below hill'. Nevertheless, the lower town should not be written off. High Street, the road from the south, is well over a mile long (sometimes it seems more, because of traffic congestion), straight and flat. It follows the line of Ermine Street, now buried a score of feet down. Just south of the city, Ermine Street was joined by the Fosse Way, the present road to Newark. The suburb through which High Street runs is Wigford, founded by the Danes as a trading depot outside the existing town.

High Street has several associations with John of Gaunt, Earl of Lincoln. In a little side-street named after him, his third wife, Katherine Swynford, is said to have had a town house on the site known as John of Gaunt's Palace, but latterly the house is thought to have belonged to the Sutton family. In any case, most of it was destroyed in the eighteenth century. Opposite Gaunt Street are the remains of the building called John of Gaunt's Stables. It has nothing to do with him but was the Hall, dated 1160, of the influential Guild of St Mary. Among what survives is the front along High Street, its façade pierced by an archway carved with leaves and flowers including honeysuckle. Through the arch is a courtyard, with a separate house, possibly Norman too. The courtyard was occupied by a carpenter's shop at the time of writing.

Near St Mary's Guildhall is the church of St Peter at Gowts, a Saxon-Norman foundation. (A gowt is a watercourse.) Nearer the river is St Mary's le Wigford, 'the oldest church in Lincoln', with its tall Saxon tower. In the street outside the church is St Mary's Conduit, a source of water in 1540.

Where the street crosses the Witham, and the Pelham Bridge

flyover for motor traffic takes its graceful leap, you can look across to the Green Dragon Inn, one of Lincoln's gabled, timber-framed buildings which have been carefully restored. Many other buildings in the city doubtless have timber work at present concealed, and it is to be hoped that they too will be renovated. Here on the Witham are Waterside North and Waterside South. Among the modern factories in this area, but mostly covered over, is the Sincil Dyke which the Romans constructed in order to reduce flooding by the Witham.

Half a mile to the west is Brayford Pool, at the junction of the Witham and the Fosse Dyke. From the shores of this mere—the pool as opposed to the hill fort in Lincoln's early name, Lindon—you can look up at the whole length of the cathedral, and across the water to a ring of warehouses, now depleted, which clearly shows how into the medieval inland port Lincoln incorporated a railway centre and then the hub of a road system. Scores of pleasure craft are nowadays anchored in this water park at the heart of the city. The Pool is also busy with working boats, for it has links with 3,000 miles of canals and rivers and with the sea.

Lincoln has established a pedestrian precinct at the foot of the bluff. Shoppers and strollers can watch whole flotillas of swans coming down the river from Brayford Pool or going up to it. They are the species called mute swans and are so many that it is sometimes necessary to control their numbers by piercing some of the eggs. Lincoln swans have been famous for centuries. When swans graced royal banquets, Henry III requisitioned 125 from centres between Lincoln and Northumberland in 1251. The keeping of swans was regulated by codes drawn up after the fifteenth century, the only surviving record being the Witham Ordinances formulated by the Lincoln Swancourt in 1524. The Ordinances kept the swans from being disturbed, for instance, and to protect them from pollution forbade the throwing of anything noxious into the waters.

At the pedestrian precinct the Witham, more like a canal than a river, is spanned by the High Bridge, a twelfth-century structure, the oldest in Britain still to carry buildings. These are half-timbered shops, three storeys high. Part of the bridge's original masonry can be seen—but, other than in exceptional circumstance, by only about half the population, as it is in an alcove down the steps marked Gentlemen opposite the shops. Happily everyone can go down steps on the other side of the street to the waterside and admire the back of the shops, almost as picturesque as the fronts. Under them the Witham glides through inky shadows, provoking the citizens' epithet, 'The Glory Hole', which is less derisory than might be thought, for beyond the dark cavern of the bridge all is dramatically light again.

Only a hundred yards or so up from the High Bridge is the archway called the Stonebow. This was the southern gate of the medieval city. The four arches date back to the fifteenth century but since then the three storeys of Lincoln Guildhall have been built round them. The Guildhall itself is on the upper floor, a great room with an open timber roof. Before each Council Meeting the Mote Bell, dated 1371, on the roof is rung. Lincoln's historic regalia are displayed in the Guildhall, including the Mayor's ring, his staff of Brazil wood, his chain of office, two maces and three swords.

After examining the Guildhall and the Stonebow as they deserve, turn your back on them and look left and right along the street on which the Stonebow fronts. You are looking along the line of the walls of the Roman town after it had been extended down the bluff. Your view is limited, left and right, by not very interesting buildings about 400 yards apart. That short stretch is the width of the enlarged Roman town.

A short distance east along this street, Saltergate, a section of Roman wall has recently been excavated, disclosing a gateway of which the existence had hitherto been unsuspected. The present street level is a good ten feet above the Roman wall, because of building and demolition and rebuilding throughout the intervening centuries.

Farther east is the Central Library, without whose resources and helpful staff no serious book on Lincoln or Lincolnshire can be written. Among the special departments is the Tennyson Research Centre, including the larger part of the poet's own library, as well as interesting mementoes.

Just round the corner from the Library is the City Museum. Its upper part is in the oldest surviving Franciscan chapel in Britain, with a timbered roof and a window from the Middle Ages. The natural history collections are there now, but between Henry VIII's reign and the end of Victoria's, the room was used as a school. Downstairs are the antiquities, especially Roman, as well as a collection of German and other armour. They are housed in the beautiful stone-vaulted undercroft, a hundred feet long, which has been the museum since 1907. Before that it was a gunpowder store, a house of correction, a school for spinning and the Mechanics' Institute.

Just around the corner from the Museum is the Usher Gallery, in the only park in the centre of the city. James Ward Usher, Sheriff in 1916, was a silversmith who left his collections to the city. Among his special interests were miniatures and watches—repeating watches, musical watches, a watch like a mandolin, another like a beetle (if beetles are set with jewels), and a variety of others. The fascinating gallery also contains paintings of Lincoln by Turner and Peter de Wint, old English glass and porcelain from Pinxton and Torksey.

The Strait and Steep Hill

It is stiff going on foot up to the cathedral from the High Bridge and the Stonebow by way of the street called the Strait—and beyond that the real climb is to come. Even the Romans decided against a direct challenge and their road, continuing High Street, seems to have veered round to slant across the face of Steep Hill, as the ascent is aptly named. If you look up Steep Hill towards the cathedral you can see how the hillside has been terraced, originally by the Romans as they extended their town, with gardens and vineyards, down towards Brayford, and again during the Middle Ages.

At the foot of the Strait the picturesque house known as the Cardinal's Hat reminds us that Cardinal Wolsey was Bishop of Lincoln in 1514-15. Next door but one is another timber-framed house, reconstructed in 1970 by the Lincoln Civic Trust and used as headquarters by the St John's Ambulance Brigade. This building is called Dernstall House, from the surrounding district known in medieval times as the Dernstall. It is sometimes said that Dernstall was a Jewish ghetto but it was not.

It was in Dernstall that in 1255 a boy named Hugh disappeared. His body was discovered some days later in a well and his death was at once declared to be a Jewish ritual murder. Time after time the accusation has been denounced—by at least two Popes and many scholars and men of good will—as a lie prompted by hatred, malice, envy and self-interest. A pogrom resulted, and a trail of faked evidence, false witness under torture, farcical trials leading to judicial murders on a large scale. In recent times the well containing the body of 'Little St Hugh' was identified for a while with one in the house now called Jews Court. In 1928 a workman came forward and explained that he had dug the well many years before for the purchaser of the premises. Visitors had been charged admission to the well, which was kept filled with buckets of water, occasionally so full that it overflowed in the street.

Hugh apparently existed. His shrine is in the cathedral and the tomb was opened in 1791 by the Dean and Sir Joseph Banks. The complete skeleton of a boy 3 feet 3 inches long was discovered and, according to one account, the body was pickled and Banks tasted the liquid.

The Jewish community was second in number only to London. Several of their houses still exist. Jews Court on Steep Hill is believed to have been the synagogue. It is now Lincolnshire and Humberside Arts' Regional Crafts Centre, the first of its kind in the country. The Centre encourages designers and craftsmen, exhibits their work for sale, and has a bookshop and coffee room.

Next door is Jew's House, of the same date, about 1180. These Norman town houses are somewhat different from the manor house at Boothby Pagnell, built a little later. Jew's House has a central doorway, monumental and decorated, leading to a passage with store rooms on each side. From the passage, access was gained to the living quarters on the first floor. The upper floor had windows but on the street there were not much more than loopholes (windows have been added). Jew's House belonged to a rich Jewess, Belaset of Wallingford, who was hanged on a charge of clipping the King's Coin. That was in 1290, the year the Jews were expelled from Britain.

Higher up Steep Hill, on one of the steepest reaches, is the medieval house known as Aaron the Jew's House, although Aaron's connection with it is unproven. Aaron was the most famous of all Lincoln Jews. He was, of course, a moneylender, almost the only occupation permitted to Jews at that time. Without Aaron's loans, Lincoln cathedral could not have been built, nor could Peterborough cathedral, nor Kirkstead abbey, Louth Park abbey, Revesby abbey and others. Without Aaron, Strongbow could not have set out to conquer Ireland for Henry II. Aaron had business interests in nine shires. His loans to Henry II amounted to more than half the income of the monarch, who was then the most powerful in Europe.

At the top of Steep Hill we have reached the site of the Roman town. It included what is now the castle and the greater part of the cathedral. The camp occupied some forty acres, an area roughly 400 yards square, which makes it comparatively small—Gloucester covered 46 acres, Colchester 108, Cirencester 240 and London 330. The camp was defended by enormous ditches up to 100 feet wide and 25 feet deep, in front of the walls. Stretches of Roman wall can be seen near the cathedral in the sunken part of the Eastgate Hotel garden, in the lane called East Bight, in James Street and not far from a school—this section, the Mint Wall, is 20 feet high and longer than a cricket pitch.

The north gate of the Roman camp survives near the cathedral as the famous Newport Arch, the only Roman gateway in Britain still spanning a main road, here Ermine Street. The round arch, once 24 feet high but now only 16 feet because the street level has been raised over the centuries, is flanked by one of two original posterns. The east gate formerly stood in what is the forecourt of the Eastgate Hotel, but this gate was destroyed in the eighteenth century, as was the south gate. The west gate was found by chance in the wall of the castle in 1836; it collapsed but there are hopes that some day it may be restored.

If you look at the pavement and roadway in Bailgate, between the castle and the cathedral, you will find that some round setts have been let-in. They mark the site where a great colonnade once stood, a sure sign that the camp developed into a town with the refinements of civilisation. The Romans indeed imported Greek and Italian marble for private houses, not only on the hill. Some houses were heated by a hypocaust like the one under the present Deanery. A former wine merchant, a Briton, traded in wine from Bordeaux. Water was brought from Nettleham and was pumped through tile pipes encased in concrete. A sewage system was installed (the Middle Ages had only cess pits). Chariot races were mounted.

Some think that the colonnade was part of a temple, others that there was a basilica. Whatever it was, the next place to go to is Westgate, where a Victorian church, St Paul's in the Bail, is being excavated. But this church is on the site of an eighteenth-century church, and in turn that one was built where there was an earlier church, perhaps Norman, and still farther back in time even a Saxon church, considered to have been the one founded by Paulinus when he preached in Lincoln and converted Blecca, the reeve, in AD 627. This would make it the oldest church in the city. Nor is this all: below the churches is the earliest major Roman building in Lincoln, occupying a very central position in the original town. Experts consider that the building had at first a military function and was later converted to civilian use, maybe as the Forum. It seems associated with the colonnade in Bailgate. Hopes are high that the story can be filled out, for the building of successive churches means that the Roman site has been undisturbed.

Lincoln Castle

Within ten years of his victory at Hastings, William the Conqueror founded Lincoln castle and was instrumental in the founding of Lincoln cathedral, the one to enforce obedience to the king, the other to enforce obedience to spiritual rule. For the castle he chose the south-west corner of the old Roman town, at the expense of 166 houses. There is no drawbridge to the castle but otherwise the eastern gateway is all you could ask as an entrance to a fortress. Once inside the castle you are faced with an incongruous pleasaunce of lawns leading to the Gothic-style Assize Courts built in 1826. On the left are the buildings built as a prison in 1787 and enlarged in 1845; their use as a jail ended in 1878, and they have housed the Lincolnshire archives but have had to be closed because of advanced decay.

Opposite, among the trees on the slopes of the mighty earthen bank, is the enormous bust of George III from the Dunston Pillar. The king's statue was the biggest work ever carried out in the artificial material called Coade Stone, used also for the lion formerly on the Lion Brewery on London's South Bank and now at the County Hall end of Westminster Bridge. When the Pillar was judged to be a danger to aircraft in the Second World War the statue was literally pulled down. Despite this rough usage, the bust was little damaged, and details on the face, for instance, appear as good as when it was new in 1810. Coade Stone seems virtually indestructible but the secret of its manufacture has been lost, which is a pity, as modern artists, with their interest in all sorts of materials, would surely have enjoyed using it.

The banks of earth which surround all six acres of the castle enclosure are up to 30 feet high; you can walk along the top of them in places and enjoy superb views of the cathedral and the city below it. In the south-east corner of the castle is a mound crowned by a turret like a rook in chess. It was added to the Norman base of the tower last century by a prison governor with a taste for astronomy and provides the modern name of Observatory Tower. From here too the panorama is magnificent.

Near the Observatory is the prison chapel, an evil place. A set of interlocking stalls, as high as a man, kept each prisoner isolated from his fellows but in view of warders and preacher.

The rows could be emptied only as one man followed another, in order. The system has been called (in Pevsner) terrifying, brilliant and devilish.

Lincoln castle is distinguished by having two mounds. The only British comparison is with Lewes, but at Lincoln the mounds are both on the south wall. The mound of the Keep, to the west of the Observatory Tower, is bigger and is thought to be later. You go up a flight of steps—an experience you become familiar with in this castle—to a shell keep built late in the twelfth century. There is no roof, but then there never was; the keep was open to the sky. Criminals (and children born in the prison) used to be buried in the keep. The last burial was in 1877, when a man was hanged for shooting a gamekeeper at Norton Disney.

The keep is also known as the Lucy Tower, after the Countess Lucy who has been referred to before. She probably had it fortified before her death about 1136. Like Thorold, whose heiress she was, her first husband, Ivo Taillebois may also have been sheriff of Lincolnshire, and Lucy's descendants seem to have claimed to be hereditary sheriffs and constables of the castle. In pursuit of these claims two of her sons, half-brothers, sided with Matilda against Stephen in their see-saw struggle. Stephen himself was captured in 1141 at the easy victory known as the Joust of Lincoln, was freed by an exchange of prisoners and retook city and castle in 1146. The barons' party held on to Lincoln after King John's death but were defeated and the city was sacked in the Fair of Lincoln (1217).

The castle was involved in siege and fighting only once more. That was during the Civil War, when the alternation of loss and recapture followed the pattern of events in Stephen's reign.

A pit-like dungeon can be visited at Cobb Hall, another tower of the castle. The tower has two storeys, each vaulted, each used for prisoners, as the iron rings for chains make plain. Some of the carvings on the walls are said to be the work of prisoners. From 1817 to 1859 the county gallows stood on the roof of Cobb Hall. From the tower you can look over the northern part of the city, including the Westgate excavations. Between the castle and the cathedral is the open space known as Castle Hill or Castle Square, with timbered houses and the excellent Regency house called the Judge's Lodgings on the corner of Bailgate.

The Bail, ruled by the constable of the castle, took up about one-third of the city round the fortress proper and inside the Roman walls. The mayor and corporation were very envious of the constable's rule and the profits he made from his special court. After the castle reverted to the crown in the time of Henry IV, the Bail remained outside the city's jurisdiction. Charles I sold the ditches enclosing the castle, and houses were built there, some of ill fame. Disputes continued until 1845, when at last the city took over the Bail.

The city had no control either over the Close surrounding the cathedral. Under Henry II the dean and chapter set up the weekly Galilee Court which, for instance, let market stalls in the Close, though no taxes were paid. There was in practice a kind of sanctuary in the Close for men liable to arrest in the city for crime. Privileges exercised by the dean and chapter were retained until, at the same time as the Bail, the Close was taken over by the city.

The Cathedral

The Close was given a defensive wall about 1285 and it was fortified a generation later. The Exchequer Gate, the main entrance to the minster yard, has three arches and three storeys, and bears a family resemblance to the castle gateway.

To the chagrin of York, William the Conqueror appointed a bishop and had him installed at Lincoln instead of Dorchester. William's first bishop was Remigius, the tiny, dark-faced almoner of Fécamp in Normandy. No doubt he was rewarded for having contributed a ship and twenty men to the Conqueror's expedition. Almost at once, by 1075 or so, Remigius began to build a cathedral. It was consecrated in 1092, shortly after the death of Remigius.

His ambitious design is incorporated in the west front you see through the Exchequer Gate. On each side of the recessed central doorway is another recess, the spread showing the size of Remigius's church. After a fire in 1141 the third Bishop, Alexander, elaborated the west front. He added a sculptured frieze above the low recesses; to the south are Old Testament scenes, in which Noah's career is prominent, interrupted by a frame showing Daniel in the lions' den; New Testament scenes are to the north. Alexander also heightened the west towers and gave the nave a stone roof.

You readily see that this is not the whole story, for the front has obviously been lengthened, out of keeping with the Norman conception. The central doorway has again been made taller, and a row of kings (later and inferior in style) is ranged over it; there is an enormous spread of lancet arcading up to the parapet, windows have been inserted, the west towers have been given turrets and spires, which bear statues. On the northern spire the figure is the Swineherd of Stow, who contributed to the cost of the cathedral the silver pennies he painfully amassed; the figure on the southern spire is St Hugh.

Hugh of Avalon (near Grenoble) had been treasurer of the Grande Chartreuse and then prior of Witham in Somerset before being made bishop of Lincoln in 1186. The previous year the cathedral had been split from top to bottom, for which an earthquake was blamed. Hugh decided to rebuild, doing away with the Norman church almost entirely except for the west front, and work began in 1192. At his disposal was a remarkable genius, Geoffrey de Noiers, who may have been English for all the French look of his name.

Geoffrey, we believe, hit on using alternating columns of dark Purbeck marble with others of paler local oolite, enhancing the play of light over the surfaces and providing contrast. He also introduced double arcades, a blank arcade of oolite by the wall and an arcade of Purbeck marble offset so that the dark shafts come in the middle of the pale arches. In the vault of St Hugh's Choir, which has been called the Crazy Vault of Lincoln, Geoffrey departed from accepted practice by using ribs not so much for strength as for decoration, producing a design which flows over the separate bays. This innovation was of immense influence on Gothic architecture.

Hugh of Avalon died in 1200, and Geoffrey about ten years later, but the work of rebuilding continued. By about 1280 the great monument of English Gothic was completed, although additions, some important, were made at intervals until late in the seventeenth century. To pay for the medieval work, peasants made contributions as well as rich men, and another source of income was the sale of indulgences.

Outside, the central tower collapsed in 1237 and was not raised (to 271 feet) until 1311, when John of Dalderby was bishop. The result has been called, more than once, the richest tower in England. It was completed by Richard of Stow, who had earlier made the Eleanor Cross at Lincoln for Bishop Dalderby. A spire was added but a storm blew it down in 1549. Those whose breath and legs hold out can climb the interminable steps—340 by a count not mine—to the top of the tower and look away to the Wash and that other great tower at Boston, or inland into Nottinghamshire. The western towers were raised in 1420 and also given spires, but these were taken down as unsafe in 1807. The bell Great Tom of Lincoln was originally in St Mary's Tower on the northwest but was recast in 1834 and transferred to the central tower.

If you enter by the west door, you can see from a gallery (special permission having been granted) the whole length of the cathedral, 481 feet, in 'Sir Joseph Bank's view', so-called because it was the favourite of that worthy. Even from the ground, however, the sight is noble, despite being interrupted by the choir screen, or rather by the organ on top of it. An earlier organ was used by William Byrd, a Lincoln man, appointed organist in 1563 when he was 20. Byrd was a steadfast Roman Catholic, a great church composer, among the chief madrigalists, and he also excelled at writing for the virginal.

Moving through the cathedral towards the Angel Choir, you will be halted by a store of riches it is possible only to indicate here.

Remigius had been buried in the nave and the site is marked by a black Tournai slab, found in the cloisters broken in two. The big square font nearby is of black Tournai marble, from about the middle of the twelfth century; there are less than a dozen like it in England, and Lincolnshire used to have a second, at Thornton Curtis. The stained glass here and in many other windows of the cathedral was made by the Suttons of Brant Broughton.

At the crossing, under the vault of the central tower, you can look into the north transept at the glory of the rose window known as the Dean's Eye. Its glass, from about 1220, is unusual in being original—Lincoln's stained glass was calamitously damaged during the Civil War. Across in the south transept is the enormous Bishop's Eye window, from the fourteenth century, but given its flowing pattern based on two leaves about a century later. Now, unfortunately, the stained glass consists of fragments.

Two small owls look from a capital of the doorway south of the choir screen. What they look at, or should do, is one of the acknowledged masterpieces of the Decorated style in England, the elaborate screen. On each side are delightful gateways to the choir, and beyond is another of the greatest works in the cathedral, the stalls of the choir, attributed to the time of John of Welbourn, who was treasurer from 1350 to 1380. There is nothing quite like them in England. They bear symbols, emblems, figures and episodes which haunted men's imagination at the time. The great majority of the stalls, mounting in rows, have not been restored. Each misericord is carved from a single piece of oak. Some subjects are the same as at Boston, which were somewhat later, and as there, are not in sequence.

Many people consider the Angel Choir at Lincoln to be the peak of Gothic in England. It was built between 1256 and 1280. To make room for it, part of the old town wall, constructed where the Romans had walled their town, had to be pulled down. So had the east end of Geoffrey's building. The reason for the extension was to provide a more fitting shrine for the remains of St Hugh, who had been canonised in 1220, his old tomb having proved awkwardly placed for the throng of pilgrims it attracted. Certain difficulties seem to have attended the work of building. A malicious little imp kept hindering progress and would not stop until an angel threw a stone, hitting his leg. The Lincoln Imp is still there, all twelve inches of him, nursing his leg, on a corbel (second from the end on the north side, I believe).

What lights the Angel Choir is the earliest eight-light window we have, or anybody else, a glorious design nearly 60 feet high. Its composition of arches and circles incorporates a feature—bar tracery—developed only a few years previously at Amiens and Rheims and quickly applied in Westminster Abbey. The window lights an array of roof bosses, claimed to be unequalled in this country, and the angels which give this retro-choir its popular name. Twenty-eight of them are carved between arches up in the triforium; beneath the angels are beautiful small heads.

The lovely Easter Sepulchre adjoins the founder's tomb of Remigius. It does seem that, after having been moved from the nave, Remigius's remains were reburied in the Angel Choir, for a pastoral staff was among relics discovered in this tomb. The coffin of Remigius, by the way, was a mere 51 inches long and 16 inches wide.

Also in the Angel Choir is the base of a shrine which once held the head of St Hugh. His head was given a shrine of its own because it had been detached from the body, but thieves stole the head in 1364. It was recovered, without the coffer which had held it, and John of Welbourn had another one made. Both shrines were ransacked in 1540, together with over 4,000 ounces of silver, 2,631 (some say only 2,621) ounces of gold, quantities of precious stones, a finger of St Catherine, a tooth of St Paul and a bone of St Stephen.

Lincoln once had no less than a couple of hundred brasses but, as the diarist Evelyn wrote, using a phrase which sounds curiously modern for 1654: 'soldiers lately knocked off most of them'. With this kind of treatment it is surprising that we still have any monuments and other 'occasions of idolatry and superstition', as someone put it for Henry VIII. Fortunately many of them have survived, naturally including those of bishops. Richard Fleming, who died in 1431, was one of several bishops who founded a chantry. On his tomb he is depicted twice, once in robes, as he would doubtless wish to be remembered as founder of Lincoln College, Oxford; and once lifeless in his winding sheet, a depiction intended to provoke startled reflections, some of which may bear on Fleming's responsibility for having John Wyclif's remains dug up, burned and scattered. The chapel has been restored as a tribute to Sir Charles Anderson of Lea.

Between the Russell Chantry and the Longland Chantry is the south portal, known as the Judgement Porch from a scene above the deeply-set door. In the roof of the archway the ornament includes a band of figures, no longer considered to represent the Wise and Foolish Virgins. Near the porch is a buttress with the gargoyle known as the Devil on a Witch's back. Edward I and Eleanor have statues on another buttress, and for long the statue on the next buttress was identified as Margaret of Valois, whom Edward married after Eleanor's death.

Lincoln cathedral had no need of cloisters, since it was not a monastery, but cloisters were added about 1290. They are connected to St Hugh's transept and contain many relics, from stone coffins to sculptures. One of several huge gravestones is that of Richard of Gainsborough, the master mason who died in 1300. The cloister is linked to the chapter house, which was built earlier.

Until Lincoln built one, England had no polygonal chapter house, but Westminster hastened to adopt the new style, and then other English places followed suit. Not all of them chose a ten-sided design, as Lincoln did. During the Middle Ages several Parliaments held in Lincoln met in the vaulted chapter house, with its central pier surrounded by ten Purbeck marble shafts. In it John of Dalderby tried some of the Knights Templars in 1310; in it Thomas Moyne read an expurgated version of Henry VIII's reply to the demands sent him in 1536 on behalf of the Lincolnshire men (an episode mentioned at Louth).

Outside the chapter house, on the lawns, is G. F. Watt's statue of Tennyson, cloaked, wearing a slouch hat and accompanied by his wolfhound, Karenina.

The cathedral's old library was burned down in 1609. In 1674 Dean Honywood paid for a new library, built 'according to Sir Christopher Wren's directions'. Sir Christopher seems to have directed a builder named Evison to build a colonnade, with the library above it. Two works from the library are now lodged in the cathedral Treasury; they are William I's charter for transferring the See to Lincoln, and a copy of Magna Carta—only three others exist, at Salisbury and two in the British Museum; Lincoln's copy has the name of the city written on the back as though establishing ownership. The Library retains medieval manuscripts, books printed by Caxton and other early printers, and first editions of *Don Quixote* and *Paradise Lost* and of part of Spenser's *Faerie Queene.* Although Dean Honywood should get the credit, the building he paid for is generally referred to as Wren's library. Incidentally, another association with Wren is claimed for a large pulpit in the nave near the black Tournai marble font; the pulpit came from St Mary's church in Rotterdam, said to have been built by Wren in 1708 for the English congregation.

After visiting the cathedral it is difficult to collect one's thoughts. Perhaps it is best to surrender to the spell of the place, as D. H. Lawrence's character Will Brangwen did in the novel *The Rainbow.* When Will entered the cathedral 'his soul leapt, soared up into the great church . . .'. On the other hand, his wife Anna 'hung back . . . she caught at little things, which saved her from being swept forward in the tide of passion, that leaps on into the Infinite.' She stood arrested before the 'wicked, odd little faces carved in stone. These sly little faces peeped out of the grand tide of the cathedral like something that knew better. They knew quite well . . . that the cathedral was not absolute . . . "However much there is inside, there's a good deal they haven't got in", the little faces mocked'.

Yet mockery in turn breeds doubts about itself, allowing another voice to be heard, that of John Ruskin: 'I have always held and am prepared against all evidence to maintain that the cathedral at Lincoln is out and out the most precious piece of architecture in the British Isles and roughly speaking worth any two other cathedrals we have.'

The bishop now lives north of the Close. Bishop Longland (1548) was the last to live in the Old Bishop's Palace. Under his successor many of the estates had to be surrendered and the bishop left the Palace for his manor house at Nettleham. Later bishops transferred to Buckden. Last century the bishops returned to Lincoln, where Bishop King modified a Georgian house into a Tudor one and used it as a new palace. That has now been turned into the Diocesan Offices and Centre. He could not use the old medieval palace because it had been dismantled while Cromwell was Lord Protector and its weed-grown walls were quarried in the eighteenth century to mend the cathedral. Hugh of Avalon had begun the Palace on the steeply-falling hillside, Hugh of Wells had completed it by 1234. The only comparison in its heyday was with Wells. Lincoln has been claimed as the biggest single planned bishop's palace. At the time of writing it is being conscientiously excavated for the Department of the Environment.

The Great Hall of the Palace was about 100 feet long and 60 feet wide. Most of it has gone but rows of pillars once divided it into aisles, and its length is marked by the east and west walls, a porch and three doorways at the south end. The middle doorway led to the kitchen, the others to buttery and pantry. Above these was the bishop's solar or Great Chamber. What is now a lawn to the east of the ruins was once a lesser hall and dining room, attributed to Bishop Alnwick in the reign of Henry VI. Alnwick also built the gate tower, three storeys high, near the Great Hall, and a chapel.

All about the cathedral are interesting old houses, some of the best being in Pottergate. On the way there you can explore the alley called Greestone Stairs. It leads from Grecian Place. Both names should be Greesen, meaning steps (singular 'gree'). Steps do indeed lead down, as steeply as Steep Hill, part of the way to Lindum Road. The narrow lane is delightful, both for the view of the town below hill and for the Georgian houses and gardens you pass, beginning with the former Archdeaconry. There is also a great tithe barn dating from 1440 and a little arch piercing the wall of the Close.

At the end of a recent visit to Lincoln, a friend and I stood on Motherby Hill, an alley which shoots rather than drops down along the top of the extended west wall of the Roman town. We could see very clearly how high the wall had been from the way the level falls outside it. Below us was the new City Hall, which can only be approached by car from the back; and at the back is a recently uncovered section of massive Roman wall. Around the City Hall is part of the one-way traffic system lapping the Stonebow. We could see to the tilted open green space of South Common, almost rural. In the middle distance were the railway yards and Brayford Pool.

There, by the Pool, my friend had pointed out the empty site of Dickinson's Flour Mill across the Pool. The Mill, which had symbolised the importance of agriculture to Lincoln, was part of an industrial waterfront, of which only Hercock's Banana Warehouse remains. Dickinson's Mill, a building listed as of special architectural and historic interest, was quickly pulled down in 1971 under circumstances which aroused controversy.

It can be agreed that the Mill and its neighbours had outlived their usefulness and that the site was needed for development. The problem is: what type of development? Already Lincoln has shared to some extent in the growth of service industries, a phenomenon of our time. A huge office block was scheduled to replace Dickinson's Mill. Voices have been raised against such schemes, which are felt to ruin all chances of preserving the city for its inhabitants and, it is hoped, an increasing number of visitors. Others point out that without developers, investors and employers, Lincoln is doomed to stagnate, 'to become a Pompeii, all ruins and no people', as one planner has said. Tourists will need hotels (on the shore of Brayford Pool, it has been suggested), car parks, traffic schemes and other measures which have to be paid for.

How Lincoln will alter was not clear when my friend and I looked down on it from Motherby Hill. It is still not clear. Changes brought about by the break-up of the old county structure will work themselves out for years to come. Some of Lincoln's problems are unique to the city; some it shares with other towns and districts in Lincolnshire and beyond.

SIX

East of the Heath

Knights, Squires and Witches

North of Lincoln, Ermine Street is also known as the A15 but the A15 south of Lincoln has no Roman connections. It makes, headlong and villageless, for Sleaford but less brutally straight than on the Cliff. It has one notable feature a few miles beyond Lincoln's southern suburbs. By the roadside a clump of trees all but hides the tower of the only land lighthouse (so it is said) to be erected. This is the Dunston Pillar, set up in 1751 by Sir Francis Dashwood, with a lantern on top to guide wayfarers across what was a particularly desolate tract. By 1810 the fifteen-foot light was evidently considered unnecessary, and the Earl of Buckingham removed it for an immense statue of George III, whose jubilee was celebrated in that year. The man responsible for erecting the statue was John Willson, who unluckily fell to his death; he was buried in Harmston churchyard. By 1940 the Pillar was a danger to military aircraft and it was shortened by removing the statue. As noted, the bust is in the grounds of Lincoln castle at the time of writing.

Some miles farther on, we turn off along a charming, lonely road between hedges—a feature of what used to be Kesteven. Our objective is the back garden of a farm, open to the public although privately owned. A fifty-foot stone tower rises in three storeys from lawns, and when I was last there a washing-line was attached to it. The tower is what remains of the Temple in the Heather, Temple

Bruer, a preceptory of the Knights Templars. This Order was founded in 1118 to protect pilgrims to the Holy Places and took its name from quarters in the Temple Convent in Jerusalem. Originally dedicated to poverty, the Templars became known for their reckless courage and presently for their wealth and influence. These earned them the bitter enmity of the king of France, who in 1307 had them suppressed, tried and often cruelly tortured. England followed suit, the Templars' property being awarded to the Knights Hospitallers. (The Hospitallers were themselves suppressed in 1540 by Henry VIII; the Order was revived in 1878 as a voluntary body, working as the St John Ambulance Brigade.)

The tower of the preceptory (later a commandery of the Hospitallers) was joined by a cloister to a round church, rare in England—the Temple Church in London is one of the few examples. Little is to be seen of the Templars' church but it has been excavated.

Still farther along, again just off the A15, is Cranwell, where the RAF College was founded in 1919, though the main buildings, surrounded by lawns, date from 1933. Beyond Cranwell, near a crossroads is a grove of trees and by it a garage facing a patch of rough grass. This is the place to look for the enormous metal horseshoes which have been put there to commemorate Bayard's Leap.

Many stories are told about this feat. In one version Old Meg the witch had her hut where the garage now stands. She blighted crops and bewitched cattle until a man dared at last to do away with her. Armed with his sword and riding his trusted horse, Bayard, he went to Meg's hut and called to her. When she came out, he slashed at her, wounding her, but she leaped up behind him on Bayard, driving her nails deep into the horse. Bayard gave three stupendous leaps, then the man turned in his saddle and killed Old Meg with a sword stroke so powerful that it also killed Bayard. Until early in the nineteenth century the hoof prints were cut out in the ground. Who put the horseshoes in place I have been unable to discover.

East of the A15 there is another road south, a sinuous route with much to commend it, including many pretty villages having a wealth of folklore concerning witches and hauntings. Near enough to be included is Potter Hanworth, where I once found the flower festival in progress, combined with an exhibition of local history. The name of the village had been presumed to indicate the existence of a pottery but it was not until 1973 that the archaeologist, Miss Hilary Healey, actually discovered local medieval pottery fragments, some of which were displayed that day.

Residents, museums and other organisations had contributed a host of items, including many old photographs collected by W. E. R. Hallgarth, whose pupils in Grimsby had compiled a history of the village. Veterinary bleeding knives, dust goggles worn during threshing, a special spade for cleaning fen dykes, skirt hooks with which ladies raised their skirts out of the mud, Victorian clothes and shop gear, a goffering iron, an apple corer made out of a chicken bone, and a chain-driven watch were among the exhibits, with harness, home crafts and many documents—one record showing how terrible a diphtheria epidemic could be last century. All this was in the school, at one end of a triangular green, where trees were banked with flowers. At the other end of the green, near the tree-shaded church, is the waterworks tower, with a meeting room below it.

At the next two villages the scale is grander. A score of generations of d'Arcys at Nocton were followed about 1530 by Thomas Wymbish, who built a Hall, and there Henry VIII is said to have stayed with Katherine Howard during his 1541 progress. Sir William Ellys rebuilt Wymbish Hall in the seventeenth century. By 1726 Sir Francis Dashwood had come to own the Hall, and in his day Nocton was the scene of fancy-dress masquerades, to which guests could be guided by the lantern on the Dunston Pillar. Great changes were introduced some years later by George Hobart, later 3rd Earl of Buckinghamshire. In 1767 he demolished the Nocton church because it was too near the Hall and presently had another one built farther away. Because the fen was too near the Hall, he set about draining it by a windmill pump.

Marriage to a Hobart heiress brought Nocton to Frederick John Robinson, later Viscount Goderich, later still Earl of Ripon. In 1834 the Hall was burned down and was rebuilt in Tudor style by the Earl. Also in 1834 Hobart's windmill pump was replaced by a steam engine of four horse-power, a mechanical prodigy capable, as it turned out, of pumping water faster than the fen could supply it. After Ripon's death in 1859 his widow had a third church built, for which she is to be congratulated, for Hobart's was not much thought of, whereas the one Sir George Gilbert Scott designed for Lady Ripon is one of his best. The RAF have taken over Nocton Hall as a hospital.

The foxhounds of the Blankney Hunt are kennelled at the far end of the estate village, a picture of stone houses, Tudor-looking but laid out before the middle of last century. Upwind from the kennels is the ruined Blankney Hall, once a great Palladian house. In its Victorian heyday Blankney was the scene of lavish entertainment, the Prince of Wales among the guests of the squire, Henry Chaplin.

The Chaplins came from Wiltshire in 1658, when John Chaplin married the heiress of Sir John Hamby of Tathwell, a pretty place near Louth. As to Blankney, it had been confiscated by Henry VIII, embellished by the Thorolds, confiscated again (from the Widdringtons) after the Jacobite rising of 1715, and bought in 1719 by Thomas Chaplin. The most famous of the succeeding squires was Henry Chaplin, born at Ryhall Hall, near Stamford, in 1841.

When he came of age in 1862 Henry Chaplin inherited 25,000 acres in Lincolnshire. Chaplin did not lavish his wealth on building a great house or on works of art but on animals—horses, foxes and foxhounds. At Christ Church, Oxford he had joined the racing and hunting set dominated by the Prince of Wales. Chaplin hunted six days a week in his prime and was out in the 1921-22 season although he had long been 'splendidly built about the haunches', as a stalker told him on the 70,000 acres he had rights over in Sutherland.

Chaplin was MP for Mid-Lincolnshire (for Sleaford from 1885) for 38 years and held various government posts; in 1907 he defeated Bertrand Russell to become MP for Wimbledon. He was a diehard Tory and a great Protectionist—not unnaturally, since his large rent roll derived from thousands of acres of wheat. His grand scale of entertaining, his hunting and racing strained his resources; imports of foreign wheat, allied to bad harvests, diminished his income. In 1892 he sold Blankney to Lord Londesborough.

The best-known episodes in Henry Chaplin's life involve his rival, the Marquis of Hastings, whom he had known since his Oxford days, a man of unstable character, a fantastic gambler and racehorse owner. In 1864 Chaplin proposed to the lady known as the Pocket Venus, Lady Florence Paget, daughter of the second Marquis of Anglesey. She accepted him although for a time she had encouraged Hastings. The wedding dress was already chosen and the couple had received congratulations from the Prince of Wales when, on 16 July 1864, Lady Florence, then aged 21, left Chaplin at the entrance to Marshall & Snelgrove's in London. She walked through the store and out on the other side, met Lord Hastings there and went straight to marry him at St George's, Hanover Square. Chaplin went stalking in Reay Forest and then for a year's tiger shooting. Lady Florence's marriage was not happy.

Chaplin took up horse racing on a large scale and a sensational rivalry with Lord Hastings ensured. The climax came in 1867, with Chaplin's entering the horse *Hermit* for the Derby. Hastings had the favourite, *Vauban.* A frantic series of wagers followed, by which a win for *Hermit* would cost Hastings £120,000 and bring Chaplin £140,000. The preliminaries to the race were full of drama. A week before Derby Day, *Hermit* suddenly coughed blood in a trial, then his jockey was claimed by another owner, leaving the almost unknown rider Daley to be engaged at the last minute. *Hermit* looked dejected and was shivering before ten false starts. At Tattenham Corner he was ninth but then Daley started a long run on the outside; *Vauban* had begun his run too early, and *Hermit* won in the last stride. Chaplin offered Hastings time to pay, and Hastings accepted, then delayed. He continued to gamble recklessly, his health collapsed and he died within a few years at the age of 26.

Lady Florence married again, and again could not find happiness. Chaplin married another Florence, Lady Leveson-Gower, in 1876, but she died five years later after bearing three children. The squire was raised to the peerage as Viscount Chaplin of St Oswald's, Blankney, and lived on to be 82, long enough to see a bird—the pheasant—all but oust his favourite animals. Edwardian house parties were as likely to revolve around shooting as hunting, and to keep up the number of pheasants the number of foxes imported and preserved could not be maintained.

Between Sleaford and Bourne

(1) *Sleaford*

It may be that holiday motorists do not always appreciate Sleaford as it deserves. They may be stuck in a traffic jam. As you approach from the south, there are level crossing gates which have a habit of being closed as you approach. In Southgate, road traffic comes in at an angle where a statue was erected in 1851 to the MP Henry Handley, a predecessor of Henry Chaplin of Blankney. Traffic lights and a T-junction in the centre of the town cause further delays.

You may be held up outside the White Hart Hotel and can see its coaching arch, or outside the Black Bull and glimpse the sign showing two dogs baiting a tethered bull. There may not be time or the desire to notice much more. Considered under more favourable circumstances, Sleaford's development turns out to be most interesting.

Only on foot can you appreciate the medieval street pattern and enjoy the unexpected winding alleyways which reveal quaint vistas and corners. The river Slea alongside Westgate is crossed by little bridges leading to the gardens of houses on its banks. Westgate also has the eighteenth-century theatre, and good architecture from the nineteenth century, some Gothic, in brick. In Northgate a beautiful little seventeenth-century house is hugged by Lloyd's Bank, and farther on is the Manor House, an extraordinary, picturesque conglomerate of materials, including stones from the castle, a medieval gateway and chimneystack, and fragments from subsequent centuries. In Eastgate the Old House dates from the seventeenth century, with stones from the castle in its garden.

The Market Place is undoubtedly where you must stand and stare. An arcade has been formed out of the Bristol Arms, once a coaching inn; the brick Lindum Hotel was given stonework as decoration early in the eighteenth century; the Vicarage has a big gable and timber-framing from the fifteenth century. Then there is the vista down Market Street, towards the Handley statue and last, or rather first, in the Market Place area is the great church of St Denys, one of the finest in Lincolnshire.

Building of the weighty tower in Ancaster stone began late in the twelfth century and the broad spire was set on it about 1220. It is one of England's earliest broach spires. The whole character of the church was altered and enriched in the middle of the fourteenth century. That was when the aisles were built, engaging with the tower so that the west front became the elaborate feature so greatly admired. From the same period is the tracery of the windows, and here is the glory of Sleaford church. The flowing patterns change subtly from window to window, culminating for many observers in the north transept. Inside, the rood screen was singled out by Pugin for special praise. The range of monuments is dominated by those of the Carre family, originally of Aswarby, their wealth deriving from wool. George Carre, who built up the fortune, has a brass of 1521, with his wife. Robert Carre (1599) has an alabaster tomb; a bigger one commemorates his son, Sir Edward, and his wife. Another Sir Robert (1682) has a black and white marble tomb chest, and lastly there is the marble bust of his son, Sir Edward, a youth of 18 at his death in 1683. Older by far than these is the stone slab, apparently a coffin lid for Yveyt, the wife of W. de Rouceby, according to the Norman-French inscription.

By the time the church was built, Sleaford was already old. In fact it is often said to be the oldest town in Lincolnshire. The Belgic Coritani of the Iron Age made a settlement important enough to have a mint at the junction of trackways converging on the ford across the river Slea. The Romans laid out north-south roads along the line of the trackways, and that they too settled by the ford is shown by finds of coins and pottery. In 1859 more than 600 Anglo-Saxon burials, with grave goods, were found during the construction of the railway from Sleaford to Boston. The Domesday survey recorded the manor of Eslafford, which was later given to Remigius for his cathedral at Lincoln. The manor house was later owned by the Lord Hussey who was executed after the 1536 uprising.

So far we have been dealing with Old Place, east of most of the present New Sleaford. The new town grew up after Bishop Alexander of Lincoln founded Sleaford Castle in the twelfth century. The castle passed through various hands, including those of the Carre family, before it was demolished in Elizabeth I's time, and most of what was left went for building stone.

In 1686 the Carre heiress married John Hervey, first Earl of Bristol, and the Carre estates have been held by the Bristol family ever since. The Carre family dominated Sleaford for most of the seventeenth century. In 1636 Sir Robert Carre founded Carre's Hospital in Eastgate, near the church, a range of almshouses for twelve poor men which was rebuilt in 1814; in Northgate, next to more almshouses, is Carre's Grammar School, rebuilt in 1834 in Gothic style; and there is Carre Street. Old Place itself was naturally part of the Carre estate.

In 1794 the Sleaford Navigation made the Kyme Eau and the Slea usable from the Witham to Castle Causeway above the town, with an extension to Greylees Pits, a section used until 1933 by a man with a flat-bottomed boat drawn by a horse. A portico of the Navigation Office still stands in Carre Street, but the company ended in 1881, ruined by the railways. For a time Sleaford was one of the major railway centres in Lincolnshire, with five lines. There was even a shortlived branch line to Cranwell in 1917, temporarily used again during the last war.

While many have praised the church of St Denys, the other great building in Sleaford is much less well known. The silhouette of the Bass Maltings, unforgettable once seen, looms up on the southern outskirts of the town. By any standards these brick Maltings are extraordinary. Completed in 1905, they are nearly 1,000 feet long, about twice the length of Lincoln cathedral. In the middle is a square tower, four storeys high, built to hold two Ruston & Hornsby steam engines. This engine house has a water tower above it, and next to it a boiler house. On each side are four detached bays, six storeys high, with a timber hood for the crane. There are cottages, mess-rooms, weighbridge and so on. An internal railway complex encircles the whole range, an engine shed at the western end.

Bass, Ratcliff & Gretton Ltd, of Burton on Trent, began operations in 1892 by boring down to a powerful artesian spring, eventually yielding 27,000 gallons of water a minute. It no longer makes Bass. The Maltings have been sold and are being used as warehouses and factories. The engines have been taken out for preservation. The designer of the Maltings should be remembered; he was Bass & Co.'s engineer, H. A. Couchman.

Sleaford is rich in vernacular building from the nineteenth century, some of it small brick dwelling houses, some of it more ambitious. Distinctive work by well-known local architects includes the Sessions House, Carre's Hospital, and probably the Gas Works' Gothic entrance and offices in Eastgate, all designed by H. E. Kendall. Kendall was also active in other parts of the county during the nineteenth century. He built Spilsby Sessions House, for instance. Sessions Houses were something of a Sleaford speciality, for another architect, roughly contemporary with Kendall, was Charles Kirk, responsible for Spalding Sessions House and, more successfully, the one at Boston. Kirk restored many churches in Lincolnshire, and built some. In Sleaford, about 1860, Kirk built a house for himself in Jacobean style, later to become the Girls' High School. Other examples of his work in the town are the Grammar School, the Corn Exchange and a wing of the Vicarage. The firm of Kirk & Parry designed Lafford Terrace (the County Offices) in Palladian style, unlike Kirk's more usual Gothic.

(2) *Churches and Turnpikes*

For those with a special interest in churches there is only one way to go from Sleaford, and that is eastwards. Lying in that direction are several outstanding churches. For instance, Heckington is among the finest in England, let alone Lincolnshire. There are those who believe that the tower and spire, though each is admirable, are not perfectly matched. Otherwise there is little but praise for one feature after another, among them the south porch, the tracery of the south window of the south transept and, even more perhaps, the tracery of the east window of the chancel. The chancel may have been built after Bardney Abbey appropriated Heckington in 1345 but more likely Richard de Potesgrave, chaplain to Edward III, was the founder. His monument in a recess is much praised. The Easter Sepulchre, however, is what most people regard as the chief masterpiece. Three sets of panels tell the Easter story, while at the

21 & 22. The humble and the proud: St Leonard's Priory, Stamford (twelfth-century) and Tattershall church (fifteenth-century)

top, among little carvings, you can discern a bagpiper and a mermaid. Perhaps the Sepulchre was made by the same artist as at Navenby and at Hawton in Nottinghamshire (the one piece in England which is sometimes held to be superior), and perhaps he made the three sedilia and the double piscina opposite.

A famous landmark at Heckington was the eight-sailed windmill dated 1830, with its great dark tower, but unfortunately this unique mill, maintained by Kesteven County Council, has recently been badly damaged by fire.

Some good judges prefer Ewerby church to Heckington, swayed maybe by its very beautiful broach spire and its setting across from a piece of grass and a village cross. Ewerby has a much admired rood screen, a medieval font surrounded by bell ropes, ten of them, a peal equalled in number in Lincolnshire only by Grantham, and a memorial to the 12th Earl of Winchilsea (1898) who did so much for Ewerby.

Heckington and Ewerby bear such resemblance to Sleaford's St Denys that all three are thought to be the work of the same fourteenth-century master mason. The rich window tracery is one feature which seems to bear out this theory. The same kind of elaborate Decorated tracery is found in the west windows at Swaton, whose church has been under-rated but is now being recognised at its true worth. If Helpringham church was not so near Heckington, it would undoubtedly be better appreciated. It has a fine position beyond a green belonging to a pleasant stone-built village. A few years ago Helpringham tower and spire were made widely familiar by being shown on one of our stamps.

Near Ewerby, and slightly north of Evedon's leaning church tower, is the site of Haverholme Priory. In 1137 Bishop Alexander of Lincoln gave land at Haverholme to the abbot of Fountains for a Cistercian foundation. The monks decided soon after arrival that the place was too swampy for their sheep ranching, so instead the bishop gave them land at Louth Park. Haverholme was then offered by the bishop to Gilbert of Sempringham, who had been his confessor, and Gilbertines took over. They sheltered Thomas à Becket in 1164 when he was fleeing from Henry II. Little now remains of Haverholme.

23. Alford's five-sailed working mill (1837)

Nothing is left of Sempringham village, just off the road to Bourne, or of its Priory, or of the great house, 200 feet long, which Lord Clinton built from the ruins of the Priory after the Dissolution. Only the nave of Sempringham church remains, and that is Norman, and described by Pevsner as 'thrilling'. In 1083 a deformed son, Gilbert, was born to the Norman knight of Sempringham, but Gilbert lived to be 106. He was canonised in 1202. In his lifetime he had attempted to widen the scope of education. He had also founded the only British monastic order, the Gilbertine which accepted both men and women in the same establishment. Gilbert set up St Mary's Priory at Sempringham in 1135, an enormous place, eventually 325 feet long. The nuns got a strip 35 feet wide along it. The canons got more. By the time of the Dissolution there were 26 Gilbertine establishments in England.

There are three roads leading south to Bourne. The oldest is the middle one. It is Mareham Lane, an ancient trackway taken over by the Romans and later called King Street. Nowadays Mareham Lane is a highway which attracts drivers in a hurry because it is typically Roman in having few bends and no villages on it, except Threekingham, which can be by-passed but should be visited.

A great battle took place at Stow Green, near Threekingham, in 870, when Earl Alfgar and Morcar, Lord of Bourne, raised a force which met the Danes who had terrorised Lincolnshire and caused immense destruction on their raid. Alfgar was killed in the fight and so, by repute, were the three Danish kings after whom Threekingham is supposed to be named. The slaughter seems to have been ghastly, for hundreds of skulls, skeletons and bones have been dug up south of the village. The origin of the name is less certain than the fact of the battle. Sometimes the spelling is Threckingham, suggesting a Saxon origin from a tribe of Threckings. On the other hand, there is a Three Kings Hotel, said to date from 869. It has a room where King John may have stayed, and the room below is pointed out as where he breakfasted before continuing his journey to Newark. Henry VIII called at the inn for refreshment, and Dick Turpin* too, and less embarrassingly, the stage coaches.

*If it wants to, Lincolnshire can claim the highwayman. He is said to have been a butcher at Long Sutton, in the Fens, before taking to crime.

Across the road from the popular inn, the Old Hall has a garden full of snowdrops and at the gate the jawbone of a whale, considerably worn. Threekingham church has a massive broach spire, perhaps twelfth century, one of those sometimes described as one of the finest in England. The village stocks are inside the church but they would never have held Sir Lambert de Threckingham (if it is he) or his wife Spayne, judging by the size of their gigantic effigies, measuring over seven feet in length. He was a judge who died in 1280. In the next century three more members of his family were given tombs, though the number has helped the tradition that these coffins, also gigantic, are those of the Danish kings.

Threckingham crossroads is exceedingly ancient; here the old trackways which were modified into Mareham Lane, or King Street, were crossed by another old track, the Salters Way, by which salt was brought inland from the coast. Stow Green, the site of the battle, has a tiny lock-up and an extremely old fair, one of Britain's oldest, for it is reputed to go back to Norman times.

The easternmost road to Bourne is the A15, which we have already met somewhat south of Lincoln. In the eighteenth century the Lincoln-Peterborough Turnpike Trust developed this road at the expense of Mareham Lane; hence the coaching villages we shall come to. The course of the A15 has more English staggers than Roman straightness.

In Aswarby park is a big mound which has been ascribed to the Danes, if not to an earlier period, though a story goes that it covers an elephant which died when a travelling circus was here about a century ago. Aswarby has the stables but no longer the Hall of the Carre family, sold in 1723 by Lord Carre Hervey to Sir Francis Whichcote. In Aswarby church it is easy to imagine heads in the box pews turning as Whichcotes entered and made their way to the dominating manorial pew. No memorial exists to the most famous native of Aswarby, George Bass, the explorer of Australia and Tasmania (but we shall hear more of him at Boston). His name, incidentally, has no connection with Sleaford Maltings; the old name for the lime tree was bass.

The coaching influence is obvious at Osbournby. The village is just off the road, and a pleasant surprise it turns out to be. You come past the church by a lane or street, which funnels out into a wide space surrounded by brick houses, a delightful place. Osbournby church is unmistakable by reason of its flat-topped tower which looks as if it had been rather brutally sawn off. Inside, long pipes go up to the roof from two enormous solid fuel boilers. Also inside, however, are about forty well-carved bench ends, with varied scenes on the poppy-heads. Paintings of Moses and Aaron led Pevsner to ask 'Are they the worst paintings in the country?' If you remember the Armada at Bratoft in the Marsh, it is a difficult question to answer.

Some miles south of Osbournby is Folkingham, another village with a great central open space, but here the main road passes right through it. Folkingham's Market Place slopes up from the eighteenth-century Manor House, built earlier for the Clintons, earls of Lincoln, to the eighteenth-century Greyhound Inn. No fewer than seven annual fairs were held in the Market Place. In his useful brochure of Folkingham, Canon F. R. Money tells how in 1816, while the butter and poultry were being sold, the Duke of Rutland's huntsmen, several abreast, swept at full gallop down the steep Market Place, riding over a poor woman from Threekingham, gravely injuring her.

Quarter sessions used to be held at Folkingham, and on the Billingborough road just south of the big village, the House of Correction was enlarged in 1825 to take a treadmill and up to 80 persons to be corrected. Only the gatehouse (privately occupied) and governor's house now remain, still a monumental affair. The same architect, Bryan Browning, built the Town Hall in Bourne. The House of Correction occupied the site of Folkingham castle, long since demolished.

John de Beaumont, the first Viscount known in England (1460), may have built the tapering tower of Folkingham's big church, worthy enough—it has been said—for a city. Apart from its size, it has a very fine rood screen and also rood-loft stairs. Some of James II's dragoons were shut up in the church in 1689 after having been taken prisoner by William III's supporter, Marshal Schomberg. The church was served for long by the Bradley family, among them Rev. Edward Bradley, who wrote *Verdant Green* under the pen name of

Cuthbert Bede. A Folkingham family perhaps better known nowadays is that of Jean Ingelow, generally associated with Boston and her 'High Tide' poem.

The famous costumier Worth was born in Bourne, though the fame attaches to his Paris days. Bourne was not the birthplace of Hereward the Wake. When the Danes tried to reconquer England in 1070 and sailed up the Ouse, the fenmen rose in support, led by Hereward, who continued to oppose William the Conqueror after the Danes had given up and sailed home. The Normans captured his stronghold of Ely, however, and Hereward then made peace, an action which has somewhat lessened his reputation. Hereward was claimed as ancestor by the de Wake family of Bourne, who had a big castle, with two moats, where Edward III was entertained. Traces remain near where the railway station used to be.

Bourne was once an important railway junction. The railway company bought the beautiful seventeenth-century building known as the Red Hall. Sir John Thimelby, of the Irnham family, had lived there, and later the Digbys. The Red Hall became the station master's house. When the railway was closed, the future of the Red Hall was threatened but local effort ensured that the building was restored and, in December 1972, Lord Ancaster reopened it. Much of the credit for preserving this fine house goes to Bourne United Charities, which have an outstanding record in providing, maintaining and extending amenities in the town.

Given the prominence of the Wakes, it is natural that Hugh de Wake should sometimes be credited with founding Bourne Abbey in 1138. An important literary figure is associated with the abbey —Robert Manning, or Robert de Brunne. He is not so important for the literary quality of his work as for its influence in helping to standardise the East Midlands dialect, which developed into the language we use today. The present parish church is the nave of the old abbey church; otherwise the abbey has gone. Candles are still used in all 24 branches of the three-tiered brass chandelier dated to 1742. A memorial to Thomas Rawnsley reminds us that during the Napoleonic invasion scare he raised the Rawnsley Light Horse Rangers at his own expense. One of his descendants, Canon H. D. Rawnsley, was a founder of the National Trust and wrote about the

Tennysons, and the Canon's brother, W. F. Rawnsley, wrote about Lincolnshire.

The town has an enviable supply of water, flooding up from the limestone to form St Peter's Pool, or Well Head, used long ago for the moats of the Norman castle. The Bourne Eau flows through the town and across the fen to join the river Glen.

Some of the best remaining stretches of the Roman Carr Dyke can be seen near Bourne, from the significantly named hamlet of Dyke in the north to Thirly church in the south. Then, as the Fens proper begin, the Carr Dyke is difficult to trace.

SEVEN

Byways of the Heath

A little to the southwest of Sleaford, near the golf course, is Rauceby Warren Nature Reserve, 25 acres owned by the Lincolnshire Trust for Nature Conservation. Most of the sandy warren which developed here in the aftermath of the Ice Ages has vanished, leaving only some heathland turf on the golf course and the nature reserve as a sample of the previous landscape. It resembles the Breckland straddling Norfolk and Suffolk in vegetation, and one plant—the smooth rupturewort—is rarely found except there and on this reserve. Excavations for sand gravel have disturbed much of the reserve but naturalists follow with interest the way plant colonies succeed each other as bare ground is turned into established turf. They also watch how the flooded pits are colonised. What is now a wood of Scots pine used to be a rubbish tip until the Trust took over.

Along the lanes southwest of Sleaford you will find some of the most charming villages of Lincolnshire. I think, for instance, of Kelby's village green, its village pond with ducks, the houses with gabled porch and mullioned windows, a yew to one side of the path to the church door, acacia on the other side. Along the lanes, straw had been machine-baled in cubes which were built up to form rectangular stacks. Some of the stacks were being pulled to pieces for fodder for the many sheep and even more cows in the fields. Farther along, a modern windmill on a sort of metal tripod contrasted with the brick tower of a disused old windmill.

Oasby has not been much mentioned in guide books, perhaps because it has no church, but it is delightful, with a picturesque inn and a charming manor house with a cedar in front of it (and no hedge or wall). Modern houses in the village have been designed in keeping, and everywhere the gardens have repaid careful tending with handsome displays.

Sunken lanes, as attractive as byways in the Wolds, wind between hedges and tall grass and cow parsley on the way from Oasby to Heydour. Fourteenth-century stained glass in two windows of Heydour church was given by Geoffrey le Scrope, prebend at that time. The Newtons of Culverthorpe Hall had their family chapel here, containing two monuments by Rysbrack and two by Scheemakers. Heydour (sometimes written Haydour) had a castle west of the church but visible traces of it are insignificant, and I was told that no written records exist—according to my informant, they were destroyed by the Star Chamber.

The lake in the park of Culverthorpe Hall almost laps the road. Parking is permitted across a causeway, and angling too, and picnickers are well aware of this nook, a peaceful place echoing to the sounds of waterfowl and providing glimpses of the great house. If too popular with others on the day you are there, go opposite to a little open grassy space on the edge of a coppice. The Hall was built by Sir John Newton around 1680 but Palladian extensions were undertaken by Sir Michael Newton from 1734. The garden was replanned just before the First World War. A private drive leads from the horse chestnuts, superb when in flower, lining the road from Swarby. Swarby church is exceptional in these parts because the massive church tower has no spire. On the triangular village green, Swarby has a little round pumphouse with a conical roof. A stream flows by, crossed by three little bridges, one with an iron handrail, one with a stone wall, one a footbridge.

In the village of Ropsley across the Grantham-Boston road, an inn is called the Fox's Brush. The name combines references to the farmers' enemy and to Ropsley's famous son, Richard Fox, born there before 1450, and for long one of Henry VII's most trusted statesmen. Fox's local importance is that he re-endowed the grammar school at Grantham, where Isaac Newton was to be educated. Fox was appointed to high offices in the church, as bishop first of Exeter, then of Wells, then of Durham and lastly of Winchester. He served

Cambridge as Chancellor of the University and as Master of Pembroke College; at Oxford he founded Corpus Christi College and was a patron of Magdalen. Under Henry VIII, Fox was ousted by Wolsey and quietly lived out his days (to 1528) at Winchester. His birthplace in Ropsley was the Peacock Inn, now greatly changed.

Although the Great North Road, the A1, is so near, the woods, the little valleys and the knolls separating them enclose a countryside which does not seem to have changed much for centuries. Yet even here, near the source of the river Glen, it is a surprise to come across a Norman house. Boothby Pagnell Manor House had a moat but otherwise no defences. Far from being a castle, it is a dwelling house, the best example in England of its type. A simple design, brick-shaped (the roof is a later addition), it has a vaulted undercroft below the hall, which is reached by outside stairs. Inside there is a very big fireplace for warmth—the house has now no kitchen; next to the hall, the living room known as the solar had no heating.

Several little roads converge on Irnham. Visitors are drawn to Irnham church for the Easter Sepulchre, now displaced but still one of Lincolnshire's finest. Brass-rubbers too come to Irnham. The family who owned the Luttrell Psalter once held the manor, and Sir Andrew Luttrell, 5th Baron of Irnham, has not only a canopied tomb but an enormous brass from 1390. A smaller brass, of a knight, nearby is thought to have been intended for Sir Geoffrey Hilton, who died about 1440, after his family had succeeded the Luttrells. The church was endangered in 1887 by a fire which seriously damaged Irnham Hall, yet another attraction for visitors when open to the public.

A Hilton heiress had married Sir Richard de Thimelby, who built the Hall soon after 1510. Subsequent alterations have left it essentially a silver-grey Elizabethan house on an ambitious scale, low but battlemented, many windowed. The Thimelbys were Roman Catholics. Despite persecutions, they held to their faith. Their priest had a hiding hole as well as another secret refuge and an underground passage leading to the garden. When John Saxton made his map in 1576 the Hall had a deer park of 224 acres, and the fallow deer were there until the First World War.

After all this, it might seem an anti-climax to go farther, but

Corby Glen can hold its own. The Glen refers to the river. The size of the market place, the presence of the market cross, remind that it has been a local centre since 1239. No more weekly markets are held, but each year there is a great sheep fair, with thousands of animals sold. Accommodation is less of a problem than in some Lincolnshire towns, for Corby has several inns. Corby castle has gone. The manor house, Elizabethan or Jacobean, as shown by its chimney stacks, became the rectory last century. The Grammar School has become the Willoughby Memorial in our time. The building, erected in 1673, was founded by Charles Reed, after whom the secondary modern school (1962) is named. The Earl of Ancaster restored the Grammar School in memory of his son, Lord Timothy Willoughby de Eresby. By an admirable arrangement, it can be used as a library and exhibition gallery.

Decoration work on the church in 1939 revealed that an almost unrivalled sequence of early fifteenth century wall paintings were hidden under whitewash. The subjects include a Nativity, St Anne teaching the Virgin, her daughter, to read, a gigantic St Christopher, the weighing of souls at the Last Judgment, the Seven Deadly Sins, the Heavenly Jerusalem, the resurrection of the dead and (a fragment) the Doom, or sounding of the Last Trump.

Between the river Glen and Bourne there is a lake. In the twelfth century Vaudey (Vallis Dei) Abbey was built south of the lake and a castle north of it. A turret called King John's Tower is incorporated into the present Grimsthorpe Castle, which was built in part of stone from Vaudey Abbey. Other parts, much grander, were Vanbrugh's last commission. Grimsthorpe is, of course, the seat of the Earl of Ancaster, Lord Willoughby de Eresby. We heard of the family at Spilsby and now resume their story.

The Duke of Suffolk who married Katherine, Baroness Willoughby de Eresby, wished to entertain Henry VIII befittingly in 1541 when the king was on his way to meet James V of Scotland. Suffolk had Grimsthorpe Castle rebuilt in haste, without proper foundations, necessitating extensive restorations by later generations. Nor was Henry's marriage more secure; the queen, Katherine Howard, was accused presently of having been unfaithful at Grimsthorpe and elsewhere, and was executed.

The son of Peregrine Bertie, Robert, was made Lord Great Chamberlain and created Earl of Lindsey by James I. He was killed, with two of his sons, in the Royalist army at Edgehill, and Montagu, second Lord Lindsey, was wounded and captured. Later, Montagu attended Charles I on the scaffold and was one of only four peers at the king's burial. It may have been Montagu who restored Grimsthorpe after it had been sacked by Parliamentarian troops.

In 1724 rebuilding began on the grand scale. Plans were commissioned from Sir John Vanbrugh by the fourth Earl of Lindsey, created Duke of Ancaster and Kesteven, who died before they were completed, but his son, the second Duke, saw work started. Then in 1726 Vanbrugh died. Only the North Front was completed to his plans, for money was lacking. Further work had to wait until 1840, when the West Front was restored in early Gothic style. When Grimsthorpe Castle is open to the public, its opulent and ducal style can be appreciated on the way to the great house, situated in hundreds of acres of parkland, where Capability Brown worked in 1772.

We can see what the principal actors in the Willoughby history looked like from the portraits at Grimsthorpe—Suffolk, Katherine, Richard Bertie, Peregrine, Robert and so down the line. Many of the portraits are by famous English artists, such as Lawrence and Reynolds and—claiming them as English—Van Dyck, Kneller and Allan Ramsay. In the State Dining Room are state chairs from the House of Lords used by monarchs and on a staircase is a Queen Anne grandfather clock which stopped at the moment of George III's death. The grandeur of the State Rooms leads to a climax in Vanbrugh's Great Hall, rising to the roof, each side a double tier of arches, a doorway at each end. Above the magnificent fireplace are paintings of the English kings who made grants of land to the Willoughby family, from William I to George I.

In Edenham church near Grimsthorpe the monuments continue and even excel the array at Spilsby. Edenham monuments begin with stone effigies from the fourteenth century, and a brass of Thomas à Becket, perhaps fifteenth century, and then come the Bertie family tombs from Charles I's reign onwards. The Earls of Lindsey are there, the third Earl having a massive black sarcophagus topped by seven busts of his family, all Roman of aspect. The Roman theme, toga and all, is continued with three Dukes of Ancester, but the fourth sits in his ducal robes. Even this great series of monuments is insufficient for more than five hundred years of history, and the churchyard too has its tributes to the family.

All round about, the lanes wind to and fro and up and down, sometimes steeply. They lead to more of the attractive Kesteven villages, some idyllic spots like the lake at Holywell (luckily just inside the county) and copses where nightingales sing and where you may find the nuthatch, a rarity in Lincolnshire except in this southwest corner.

EIGHT

From Grantham to Stamford

Ancaster Stone

Near Ancaster Gap, the major break in the limestone south of Lincoln, are the famous stone quarries. The stone was used in the rebuilt House of Commons, St Pancras station, St John's College chapel at Cambridge and widely for buildings in Lincolnshire.

Stone Age hunters squatted round a hearth found at the Gap; at Honington, above it, are two ditches and three ramparts, man-high, of the main Iron Age camp in Lincolnshire. Down on the floor of the Gap, below the Heath, the Romans founded Causennae, which we know as Ancaster. It was their only station on the way to Lincoln after the one at Great Casterton near Stamford.

Causennae prospered. Hundreds and hundreds of Roman coins have been discovered, 2,000 in one hoard. Tradition has it that chariot races were held on the level floor of the valley. Grantham Museum now has the sculptured Mother Goddesses from Causennae, the altar and the milestone which date from Constantine's reign. There was a local pottery. A mosaic pavement has been found. Near Ancaster Hall you can see a piece of Roman wall seven feet thick, and near the church more ramparts and a ditch as wide as a cricket pitch. The defences seem to have been added, enclosing all nine acres of the station, in the fourth century. After the Roman occupation, the cemetery was used by pagan Saxons for their cremated dead. For a long period, until the Middle Ages, Ancaster was deserted. The present village, much of it spread along a street which is Ermine Street, quite naturally has been built of local stone.

A very handsome stretch of road continues from Honington to Grantham. On the way it passes the Thorold seat at Syston and then we come to Belton.

Many visits will not reveal all there is to see at Belton, which is a complex of great house, church and model estate village. Most of the stone cottages were built about 150 years ago in Tudor or Jacobean style, grouped round the village cross and incorporating almshouses, school, smithy and an obelisk fitted with pump and trough. The church, partly Norman, has a font sculptured strangely with figures varied enough to make up a plotless drama. Nave, chancel and transept chapel are rich with monuments, some small but touching, some imposing, to the family which made Belton the fascinating place it is. Certain monuments are to Brownlows, others to Custs, as is natural when we consider the family history.

Belton manor was mentioned in Domesday but the part of its story which concerns us begins in 1620 when it was bought by a lawyer, Richard Brownlowe. For 47 years Prothonotary of the Court of Common Pleas, Brownlowe thriftily invested in land, mainly in Lincolnshire. The Old Manor House he acquired at Belton was replaced by the present Belton House about 1689 by his great-great-nephew, Sir John Brownlowe, M P for Grantham. In 1695 Sir John and his wife entertained William III. The marriage was childless, and so was that of a nephew who succeeded, John Brownlowe, made Viscount Tyrconnel in 1719. The estate passed to his sister Anne, whose husband was Sir Richard Cust. Their son, Sir John Cust, was Speaker of the Commons from 1761 to his death in 1770. It was the Speaker's son who was raised to the peerage in 1776, taking the title of Baron Brownlow. Bringing the story nearer to our times, the 3rd Earl Brownlow was Lord Lieutenant of Lincolnshire for over fifty years and was aide-de-camp to Victoria, Edward VII and George V.

From the church containing the gallery of family monuments it is a short walk through the park, past the glass Orangery which Sir Jeffry Wyatville built in 1811 and which is now the Camellia Cafe for visitors, to the rose garden and terrace below the north front of Belton House. Or you can approach through wrought-iron gates, down a mile of drive set about with trees, watching as you go for deer and black sheep (black as to coat). Above the archway leading to the courtyard is a cupola with a large old clock. The kitchens used to be on the far side of the courtyard. They measured 100 feet by 50 feet and were connected to the house by an underground railway which still exists.

Someone described Belton House as 'austere without and elegant within'. Some masonry from the Old Manor House was used when building began in 1685 but what you see is Ancaster—or rather, Heydour—stone, now mellowed from yellowish to grey. Nobody knows who designed Belton, or who built it, but he was evidently greatly influenced by Sir Christopher Wren. High above the roof, the cupola is topped by a weathervane with the Brownlow crest, a greyhound. When James Wyatt made certain alterations in 1777 he removed the cupola but the 4th Lord Brownlow restored it.

Inside, the tone is set at once by the Marble Hall, with its black and white marble floor, its Lely and Reynolds portraits (including Sir John Cust, the Speaker), and Grinling Gibbons carvings. In the Red Drawing Room are Van Dyck's painting of a white horse, Marie Antoinette's fire-irons, a Titian and a Rembrandt, and a Gioconda from Sir Joshua Reynolds's collection.

Other rooms contain masterpieces of furniture, tapestry, paintings, porcelain, silver and fittings by a long succession of great craftsmen. Even lock plates on the doors are works of art, bearing the Brownlow greyhound symbol. Lord Brownlow was Lord in Waiting to Edward VIII and among the heirlooms in the Library are unique mementoes of the king's brief reign. From the Chapel Drawing Room you can look up the long avenue of trees to the hill which bears a tall, elaborate arch of brick, the Belmount Tower, built in 1750 for Lord Tyrconnel. House and setting are indeed of a piece, and happily they are open to the public for much of the year.

Grantham

The roof of Belton House is one of many places from which you can see the supremely graceful spire of St Wulfram's church in Grantham. In the busy town, made ruddy-faced by much brick, the great church is unexpectedly revealed down a street, above seventeenth, eighteenth-century and more recent buildings, or round a corner. Grantham spire is often named with Louth and Boston Stump as among the most satisfying in Lincolnshire and in England.

Grantham is one of the few Lincolnshire towns (Lincoln, Stamford and Louth are others) to be mentioned in Domesday. From Edward the Confessor's time until 1660 the royal manor of Grantham was customarily given to the queen; thus Henry V gave it to Katherine of France, and Edward IV gave it to his mother, Cicely, Duchess of York. Edward visited Grantham himself and contributed financially to the Grammar School. It was he who granted the charter of incorporation in 1467.

The town prospered while the wool trade flourished, its merchants adding to the splendour of St Wulfram's. Destruction during the Wars of the Roses was overcome, as were setbacks in the Civil War, when Charles Cavendish took it for the Royalists and Cromwell took it back for Parliament. As it was on the Great North Road, many travellers came to Grantham, some illustrious like King John of France, who slept there in 1359 on his way to imprisonment at Somerton Castle, and Henry VII's daughter, Margaret Tudor, as she went to marry James IV of Scotland. The coaching era benefited Grantham, a staging point at the foot of Gonerby Hill, which as readers of *The Heart of Midlothian* recall, was a terror to horses. Grantham was a market town, with watermills like the Swallows Mill, and well known for breweries, some of the maltings only nowadays disappearing.

A change was marked by the construction of the thirty-mile canal from Nottingham in the 1790s, a costly venture to finance but one which soon paid well. Its making encouraged the building of factories near the wharves. In 1852 the Great Northern Railway came to Grantham, after having overcome the difficulties of crossing the Heath. When railway engineering works were later established, Grantham became more and more an industrial town. Recently Grantham has concluded an arrangement like Gainsborough's with the Greater London Council for the introduction and development of new industries.

While locomotives were being changed at Grantham station it has been known for the driver and the guard to slip off and buy pies

24 & 25. Peace and oppression: Norman ruins of Croyland Abbey, founded in 716, and the grim brick keep of Tattershall Castle, mid-fifteenth-century

from one of the pork butchers for which the town is noted. Grantham is also noted for its inns. In High Street there is the George, 'one of the best inns in England', Dickens called it in *Nicholas Nickleby.* It occupies the site of a hospitium for travellers mentioned in Edward IV's grant of the manor to his mother. The old building was demolished in 1780. The present brick inn (given its name, it can hardly be anything but Georgian) was in its early days a favourite meeting place, for it had its own theatre.

Opposite the George is the Angel and Royal Hotel, a superb example of a medieval inn. Doubt has been cast on the story that King John held a court there in 1203 but a building seems to have existed in the twelfth century. The Knights Templars owned it and provided shelter for travellers, as did the Hospitallers after them. The façade on the street today dates from the fifteenth century. An arched gateway is flanked on one side by a head identified as that of Edward III and on the other by the reputed head of Philippa, his queen. Above the gate an oriel window is supported by a corbel, and above that the front has a decorated parapet. Inside, at street level and on the first floor, enough medieval work remains to make it easily understandable how in 1483 the Angel was sufficiently important for Richard III to sign and seal there the death warrant of the Duke of Buckingham.

No castle now exists near Castlegate but in that street is a very well known sight, the living sign of the Beehive Inn—an occupied hive.

A monumental conduit in the market place confirms the importance of the wool trade to Grantham. The Grey Friars, themselves interested in wool, had provided the town with water about 1314, bringing it from springs at Gonerby. Water is now discharged from a ram's head on the conduit, built in 1597, and the symbols of Grantham wool staplers are displayed.

Grantham had an Eleanor Cross, for the first stage of the queen's funeral procession in 1290 ended there. It used to be claimed that the cross had been put up in the market place but this is not so. There is, however, the market cross, or part of it. When the Tollemache family were lords of the manor they removed the cross but it was replaced, so they took it away again, only to have it once

26. Norman chancel arch of Whaplode, among the best of the Fen churches

more, and finally, restored. Like Louth, Grantham has a street called Westgate, but instead of town houses in it, Grantham has shops full of character in the narrow part opening off the market place, and cottages where it broadens out.

Where the Eleanor Cross did stand, until the Civil War which destroyed it, was St Peter's Hill (beyond the Beehive Inn), a rather charming little green oasis with trees. Frederick Tollemache, MP, still has a Victorian statue there, and so does Sir Isaac Newton. They stand near the distinctive Town Hall, also Victorian. William Watkins of Lincoln built it to replace the old Guildhall which, after enlargement in 1787, had an assembly room where monthly meetings were held, some of them attended by the poet Goerge Crabbe, who was rector (if not always in residence) for 25 years at Allington in the neighbourhood.

Close to the Town Hall are the Library and the Museum, one of the best in Lincolnshire. The exhibits are of great interest and they are well displayed. Some of them explain Grantham's development as a community, with emphasis on its social and economic bases. Items concerning Sir Isaac Newton are included. Other exhibits illuminate the long history of the surrounding district. You can ask to see one of the specialities of the Museum, its Bronze Age collection. The Roman section has an unusually wide range, from art objects like the Ancaster sculptured goddesses to industrial finds such as the furnace used for smelting ironstone at Colsterworth.

Three other buildings form the core of the visitor's Grantham, the church, the Grammar School and Grantham House, all close together. Now National Trust property, Grantham House belonged to the Hall family. Its hall, where Margaret Tudor lodged, is older than 1400; then there was rebuilding and enlargement of the house in Elizabethan times, as shown by the look of the west front and the date 1574 on a chimneystack. Further extensions, those of the eighteenth century being major works, have followed right up to our time.

In common with Watkins's Town Hall, the Grammar School has a high-pitched roof, but the school is of course far older. Bishop Fox built it towards the end of the fifteenth century. There had been a school long before, ever since 1322, when—as seems likely—Walter

Pigot was the master appointed by Lincoln. The school Fox built and re-endowed is a double building, comprising school room and the master's house. William Cecil, later Lord Burghley, was a pupil and another, the most famous, was Isaac Newton, who lodged with an apothecary 'next to the George Inn northward in High Street'. The name has been changed to King's School, and modern buildings have been provided, but parts of the old school are still used.

The school is in the shadow of the church. For a good view of St Wulfram's it is best to withdraw a little, into Swinegate, off High Street, say, so that you can see the spire and the west front. This is the sight that so impressed John Ruskin, whose sharp eye, after taking in the grand design, picked out a resemblance to medlars in the globular ball-flower ornament so lavishly used. The tower mounts up past arcadings and bands of quatrefoil to the twin windows of the third stage and those of the fourth, where they are grouped in a single arch. Following the buttresses up, but not to the pinnacles they end in, your glance passes the belfry, with ten bells. The tower is 140 feet high, and the spire a little more, its outline slightly fuzzy with crockets.

Six Norman pillars remain in the nave but the very early church was rebuilt at the end of the thirteenth century according to a bold scheme, by which a new church was created outside the existing one. Rich patrons made money available for the engaged aisles, the chapels (one to the Hall family), the north porch, the double vaulted crypt and other features. Under an altar in the crypt, which used to be called a charnel house, the relics of Wulfram, Archibishop of Sens, are thought to have been stored. They were later kept in a room above the north porch.

In a room over the south porch is the library bequeathed in 1598 by Francis Trigg, rector of Welbourn, many of the books still chained. The oldest is a law book from Venice printed in 1472. Another library was presented by a seventeenth century dean of Rochester, Dr Newcombe.

St Wulfram's is sometimes said to be relatively poor in monuments. Perhaps it is, considering its size, but there are medieval tomb recesses to Richard de Salteby and his wife and to John Harrington. The sailor William Cust (1747) stands above a warship,

William Thorold (1808) turns his pale face in profile, and Edmund Turnor has been standing since 1769. The biggest monument and the best (though that does not always follow) is to Sir Dudley Ryder, Lord Chief Justice (1756). All these are lighted by the series of fourteenth-century windows, some with geometrical tracery, some with curvilinear, which play so large a part in making St Wulfram's memorable.

By the Great North Road

Near Grantham is one of the biggest houses in England, Harlaxton Manor. In its history an infant heir falls from his nurse's lap into the fire and is burned to death, an heiress is stolen by gipsies (or is discovered selling gloves in a London shop), families intermarry and take new surnames or discard them, lines die out and unexpected successions occur.

From the road on high ground, the long drive leads down into the valley and up, past enormous walled gardens, to a gatehouse fit for a prince of the Renaissance, which sets the scale and style. Harlaxton Manor has towers, turrets, cupolas, cliffs of windows, arches, bays, gables and chimneys combined into a gargantuan, baroque, Jacobean, Michelangelesque, theatrical pile (the adjectives are Pevsner's). The architect, Anthony Salvin, was only 32 when he designed Harlaxton. Its owner was Gregory Williams, who preferred to be known as Gregory Gregory. By 1827 he had sought inspiration in country houses from Burghley to Montacute, from Wollaton to Audley End. Then for twenty years he spent £10,000 a year on a house for himself. He may never have lived in it.

Harlaxton's bizarre story has been lucidly traced as far as 1938 by Sir Charles Welby of Denton, whose family and Gregory's were connected by marriage. In 1937 Harlaxton was bought for £70,000 by the eccentric Mrs Violet Anne Van der Elst, the vociferous opponent of capital punishment, who had reputedly made a million pounds out of Shavex, soap, face creams and other cosmetics. She renamed her purchase Grantham Castle, added seven bathrooms to the one which Gregory Gregory had managed with, and brought in twenty miles of cable to equip fifty rooms with electric light. She bought tapestries, statues, furniture, carpets and fittings from various sources, including Buckingham Palace.

Mrs Van der Elst's stay was not free from troubles, among them difficulties with Kesteven Agricutural Committee, who took over 300 acres of her land for farming in 1946. Aggrieved, the lady decided to leave England for Ireland. The Jesuits bought Grantham Castle for £50,000 as a training college for priests. Many of the contents were sold by auction, often at disappointing prices. Two weeks before Mrs Van der Elst died in 1966 the Jesuits rented Harlaxton Manor, as it had again become, to Stanford University. In turn, Stanford has been succeeded by Iowa University. Harlaxton was the location for the film *The Ruling Class.*

While Salvin was responsible for the exterior, the interior was designed by William Burn. It is equally inspired, equally imposing. Burn provided a Baron's Hall, a Tapestry Gallery and a ballroom all along the south front. Burn was not responsible for the black and purple decor of the room where Mrs Van der Elst held séances, but he was responsible for the contrasts with shadows as light floods down a staircase unique in its way. It goes overwhelmingly up past three floors. Scrolls, columns, kneeling slaves, naked little boys, mirrors, balconies and landings tower up to a blue artificial sky. On the first floor, sham curtains and swags of fruit are held by real rope, whitewashed to look artificial. Higher up, two figures of Father Time hold real scythes.

After writing about Harlaxton, Sir Charles Welby must have been thankful to return to Denton. The Welby family moved to Denton from Moulton in the Fens during Tudor times. In 1653 a set of almshouses were built in the park, their ends fancifully gabled, their joint roofs supporting a row of six chimneys. Overlooking the long lake in Denton Manor park is the grotto of the spring known as St Christopher's Well. The church too overlooks the lake. In the south aisle Richard Welby has a life-sized monument from 1714 and an inscription to his estimable character (confirmed by his pose and expression). A new hall for the Welbys was built in 1962.

South of Denton the land reaches heights unmatched in Lincolnshire except in the Wolds. The Nottingham and Grantham canal had to use locks to rise to over 200 feet just beyond Denton reservoir, a favourite place for anglers. Near Hungerton a height of 468 feet is reached, but then the land falls away northwards, overlooking the Vale of Belvoir.

At Stoke Rochford, a few miles from Harlaxton down the A1, a house was begun in 1841 to rival Gregory Gregory's Manor. The idea was Christopher Turnor's. He called in William Burn, who had been so successful with the interior of Harlaxton. Burn chose a fine site overlooking the Witham valley and designed an ambitious latter-day Jacobean house, rich in gables and turrets and chimneys, bringing off excellent effects inside, but Stoke Rochford is not as overwhelming as Gregory's monstrous home. Perhaps that is as well. Burn was also called on to lay out an estate village, for which he chose a Tudor style.

On the other side of the A1, the Cholmley family built Easton, a Victorian country house, to rival Stoke Rochford Hall, but it has gone, though the terraced gardens along the Witham remain, in picturesque neglect. Sir Henry Cholmley (1641) has an unusually grand monument in the Easton chapel of Stoke church. The church also has a Stoke chapel, with an imposing monument to Sir Edmund Turnor (1707) and other Turnor monuments. Stoke has a long history, beginning with the Romans and illustrated from the fourteenth century by monuments in the church. In our time Stoke Rochford Hall has been taken over as a College of Education, and buildings have been added.

While at Stoke Rochford, Burn put up an obelisk sixty feet high in honour of Sir Isaac Newton. Across a mineral railway line at Colsterworth is the hamlet of Woolsthorpe and the National Trust property of Woolsthorpe Manor. Here Isaac Newton was born on Christmas Day, 1642, some weeks after his father died. The house is open to the public on certain weekdays (never on Sunday). The bedroom where Newton was born can be visited, as can his study and the kitchen. In the orchard is a descendant, we are assured, of the tree from which Newton saw the apple fall, according to his stepniece, Mrs Conduitt, who told the story to Voltaire sixty years later.

As a boy Newton went to school at Skillington (in 1865 the vicar, Charles Hudson, joined Whymper's ill-fated expedition to climb the Matterhorn and was killed). Newton was also at Stoke school, and when he was 12 he went to Grantham. His mother had remarried but was again widowed and had to take Isaac from school to help with the farm and sell produce in Grantham market, a task he was liable to avoid. When he was 18 an uncle, William Ayscough, rector of Burton Coggles, enabled him to go to Trinity College, Cambridge.

In 1665 plague closed the college on and off for nearly two years and Newton retired to Woolsthorpe. During this period he began much of his greatest work, ranking in scientific importance with Darwin's. His laws of motion, gravitational theory, invention of the calculus, discovery of the binomial theorem and experiments with light—all dating from this Woolsthorpe interlude—enabled Newton to advance our knowledge of matters including mathematics, optics, dynamics, physics, astronomy and navigation, and have stimulated further developments even when his theories have been modified—by Einstein, for instance.

Stamford

Six churches, eight ancient monuments, 320 buildings of architectural or historic importance, plus 120 others on the supplementary list; these go to make up Stamford, the first town (in 1967) to be scheduled a conservation area. There are no suburbs as you approach from the south. Instead, the bank of the river Welland is fringed with meadows, from which there is a lovely view of the town. There is another view, if anything finer, from the Stamford parish of St Martin's across the Welland (not in Lincolnshire, to be honest), as you go down the fine town street, past the quaint bottle Lodges of Burghley House. From the street you have a panorama of Stamford banked up on the other side of the river. To visit nearly all the best features needs only a short tour on foot. The time needed to appreciate them is of a very different order.

The first impression is of Georgian excellence but a more ancient past is almost immediately apparent. Just east of the bridge leading to St Mary's Hill (the Georgian vista) the ford is still visible that gave Stamford its name—the Stone Ford—a prehistoric crossing on the Jurassic Way. Somewhat west of the bridge is the ford used by the Romans when they laid out Ermine Street, part of its course to be seen on the Lincolnshire side. The Romans developed the manufacture of pottery, for which Stamford was renowned over a very long period.

In the Meadows, a car park has been laid out where the remains of the castle motte stood until 1935. The first castle was Danish. The Danes had taken Stamford from Angles who settled there, but did not exterminate them. Control passed to the English after victories by Alfred the Great's successors. Stamford had an English castle, and from 972 until 1066 an important mint. The Normans in turn built a castle and under them, Stamford experienced another period of prosperity. Going up St Mary's Hill you come to the Packhorse Arch, which is really what is left of a Norman house. The street level has been built up over the centuries, as is clear from the antique shop at No. 13, where you will find a thirteenth-century crypt or vault, part of a monastery.

Stamford's wealth was increased through the power of religious houses which were established there. The earliest of them was St Leonard's Priory, now towards the eastern end of the town, founded in 1082 as a cell of Durham Abbey. The surviving west front is from the twelfth century. Partly thanks to the monks, Stamford has a venerable tradition of learning. According to Merlin of Caledonia, writing in AD 570, a university was founded at Stamford by the British Prince Bladud in 863 BC. One does not lightly contradict Merlin but no vestige of this foundation has come to light. During the Middle Ages Stamford did nearly have a university, as shown by the door knocker at Stamford Grammar School. It is a replica of the knocker of Brasenose College, Oxford. Dissatisfied students from Oxford and Cambridge left the old universities in the thirteenth century and tried to set up rival institutions in various towns. Some came from Northampton to Stamford in 1265, and more in 1333-4, establishing a Stamford Brasenose as a collegiate hall. The movement was suppressed, not without difficulty, before a university could be founded in Stamford. Only Brasenose Gate remains. The original knocker was returned to Oxford in 1890.

Stamford School was first mentioned in 1309. Alderman William

Radcliffe re-endowed it in 1530 and Lord Burghley, a former pupil, saved it from being done away with in Edward VI's reign. The School Chapel originally formed part of St Paul's church, a twelfth-century foundation.

In the Middle Ages Stamford had no direct lord but was under the king, and the dukes of York held it. In 1460 the Lancastrians, temporarily victorious, captured the town and caused much destruction. Despite this, the fifteenth century was in general another highly prosperous time. Stamford had gained enormously from the trade in wool and wool cloth. Stamford Fair was first mentioned in 1200, and its cloth became famous throughout Europe for centuries. It is said to have been used on the Field of the Cloth of Gold devised by Wolsey for Henry VIII.

The name of callis (from Calais, where the staple was) is applied to the Stamford almshouses which were founded by merchants, the most renowned being William Browne. In 1475 Browne, who was alderman on six occasions and three times Sheriff of Rutland, built the hospital of All Saints, better known as Browne's Hospital. This exceptional building stands in Broad Street, where the reprehensible bull-running was held from 1209 until 1839. The Hospital is built round a court. The original cubicles of the common room on the ground floor have gone but their positions are marked. The chapel has a screen, stalls with misericords, the original altar slab and stained glass with figures whose haloes are jewelled. Above is the Audit Room.

William Browne and his brother John restored All Saints Church, which retains much thirteenth-century work, after the Lancastrian attack. The brothers, and other members of the Browne family, have brasses in the church, William's and his wife's being nearly five feet long.

Once Stamford had sixteen churches but only four of them remain in the Lincolnshire part of the town. St Martin's, with the first Lord Burghley's Renaissance tomb, is not in our county. The tower and spire of St Mary's, Stamford form part of the lovely view from the bridge; it is sometimes called the Mother-Church of Stamford. St George's owed much to William of Bruges, the first Garter King of Arms, who during the fifteenth-century restoration presented windows showing the first 25 Knights of the Garter. Only one head survives but a record of them is preserved on the walls. Moreover, in 1732 a glazier named Exton collected some 200 mottoes of the founder members of the Garter and incorporated them in the north chancel window. Eighteenth-century monuments to members of the Cust family have been erected, and there is a plate of bell metal to Tobie Norris (died 1626) of the bell-founder family famous for their bells in Lincolnshire and other counties. Perpendicular like St Martin's, but smaller, and mainly contemporary with Browne's Hospital, St John's Church is famous for the statues of angels in the roof, one of them ringing handbells. A useful description of them is provided. Once there was also St Michael's church in High Street, a nineteenth-century building, disused and at the time of writing planned to become a shopping arcade.

A decline in Stamford's fortunes did not prevent the rise of the Cecil family in the sixteenth century. William Cecil, Lord Burghley, was Elizabeth I's Principal Secretary of State, a man rich and powerful enough to build for himself what has been called the largest and grandest surviving building of his time, Burghley House. The great landowning family dominated Stamford for three hundred years.

In the Civil War Stamford had Royalist sympathies but was held for Parliament. Cromwell took Burghley House and destroyed the Eleanor Cross, among other damage. Charles I had been at Stamford in 1633 and 1634, and he paid his last visit in 1646. It was his last visit anywhere as a free man. A fugitive, in servant's guise, he came in secret and was admitted by Alderman Wolph into his house in Barn Hill. Next day Charles left to give himself up to the Scots at Newark; they handed him over to Parliament. When the Stuart fortunes revived with the restoration, Stamford revived too, thanks this time to increased river traffic and improved roads.

Much of the Stamford we see dates from the period now ushered in, that between Bunyan's Pilgrim and David Copperfield. The local building stone and the tradition of working in it help to give unity to the houses and shops, their elegance of fronts, porches and doors tempered by the picturesqueness we find in roof-line and window-shape and the contrast with the abundance of lanes no more than passageways, offering a glimpse down to the Welland or opening on to a street packed with treasures of domestic and public architecture.

The town had profited from being near the Great North Road ever since the twelfth century, when the road was moved eastwards towards Stamford. For long, however, travellers had to go on foot or on horseback. Even during the eighteenth century the Great North Road was only a narrow paved causeway with an unmade road on either side. Strings of thirty or forty packhorses used the causeway. Coaches did not run all the year round until well after the Turnpike Trusts were established in the middle of the eighteenth century. The first coach of the season, seldom as early as May, was decorated with ribbons and flowers, and set off from Stamford preceded by the town band and young people in couples. Wheeled traffic did increase, however, after turnpike tolls provided funds for improving the roads.

The peak year for coaching was 1830, when forty mail and thirty stage coaches passed through Stamford each day. Sixty-five public houses then existed. Many of them were connected with a particular trade, as the Carpenters' Arms and the Sawyers' Arms. The Red Lion had good stables but no back way, so horses had to come in and out by the front door. Great herds of cattle passed through Stamford on their way to London, and the inn called the Parting Pot was situated where the roads to Bourne and Market Deeping divide in St Paul's street; here the cattle dealers and drovers used to meet and have a last drink before setting off again.

The George in St Martin's was the most famous coaching inn. It has been a place for travellers ever since the days of the Hospitallers. As you enter, the room on the left is marked London and was where southbound travellers waited. The York room opposite served travellers going north. The Stamford Hotel was begun in 1810 but not finished until 1829. It offered 'elegant and superior accommodation', a ballroom and dining and card rooms, and it was also a Whig centre, encouraged by the Earl of Gainsborough, to counter the George, which was Tory.

The end of the coaching era seemed disastrous to shopkeepers and others in Stamford, it being thought that the railway would drive coach traffic from the Great North Road, with consequent loss of trade. Others succumbed to the railway fever. For about eighty years after Stamford had its first line—to Peterborough—in 1846, the railways proliferated and offered many advantages in passenger and freight services, although waterborne traffic suffered.

The *Stamford Mercury* is claimed to be the oldest English newspaper to have been published continuously under the same title. It seems to have been started in 1695. About a century later, the *Mercury* attained the highest circulation outside London. That was under Richard Newcomb, from Billingborough, and his son, also Richard. The *Mercury* was printed in Stamford until 1970. It retains offices there, now at 33 Broad Street. Until 1962 these premises were the Roebuck Inn, built in 1704. The cellars remain but the stabling has gone, and so have the chaff-house, manure pit and coach house.

In 1718 a theatre was built in Stamford on a site which has not been identified. Fifty years later it was succeeded by the little Theatre Royal. An Irish eccentric comedian named Whitley formed a company which gave the first performance and went on to tour other towns, including London, thereby attracting famous players, including Macready, Kemble and Edmund Keane. The railway killed the venture by offering cheap trips to London and the theatre had to close in 1871. Now the Theatre Royal has been incorporated into an Arts Centre with the former Assembly Rooms.

One or two other public buildings have changed their function. The Library in the pedestrian precinct of High Street also houses the Museum but when the building was put up in 1804, with a portico which has been seen to owe something to the Covent Garden church by Inigo Jones, it served a very different purpose; it was the Shambles. Then in Broad Street, opposite Browne's Hospital, is a cinema. It used to be the Corn Exchange, the second one, burned down in 1924. The biographer of Sir Malcolm Sargent—like Sir Michael Tippett a native of Stamford—tells us that some time before 1920 during the children's film shows on Saturday afternoons 'Malcolm would . . . sit by Harold Rudd at the piano and help "fit" the films with the music, which they extemporised in part'. That cinema was part of the Oddfellows' Hall in All Saints Street.

In 1809 the heaviest man ever known in England died suddenly at the Waggon and Horses in St Martin's. Daniel Lambert was only five feet tall but his body was 9 feet 4 inches round, his leg 3 feet 1 inch, and he weighed 52 stone 11lb. The George has his walking stick and a portrait, and the Town Hall some of his clothing. Born in Leicester, Lambert had to retire from being Keeper of the Bridewell there because of his already enormous weight, although he ate little and drank only water. He had been exhibited in Piccadilly, London and was passing through Stamford when he died at the age of 39.

Of the great changes which have taken place in Stamford during the present century, some will strike even the casual observer. The Stamford that visitors know is almost entirely given over to shops and historic architecture. Not very many people live in the streets which make Stamford a show-place. It was not so up to our time. The centre of the town was picturesque with courts and alleyways but they were overcrowded, and tenements had been squeezed between grand houses of the middle class. The slums have been largely cleared. New dwellings have been built to the north of the old town.

Between the wars, motor passenger and goods traffic built up on the Great North Road and it had to pass through the narrow, winding streets of the town centre. Attempts to relieve the congestion by widening streets, sometimes ingeniously, were insufficient. A by-pass on the A1 was desperately needed. At last, in 1960, it was opened. Since then, however, problems have again arisen because traffic has increased still further, much of it going through Stamford on the way to the holiday coast and the Fens.

NINE

The Hollow Land

The Fens: according to William of Malmesbury: 'A very paradise and a heaven for the beauty and delight thereof'; according to Daniel Defoe: 'The sink of thirteen counties'.

A Matter of Drains

If you turn south past the general store in New York you will come after a few miles to Bunker's Hill. As the name implies, you climb up to Bunker's Hill, but only a matter of about twelve inches, from nine feet above sea level at New York to ten feet. This is typical of the Lincolnshire Fen country, the whole of it lying below the level of high tides in the Wash. When the Fens around this New York were drained about two hundred years ago, small settlements were founded, and in choosing a name, North American places then in the news provided inspiration. Any resemblance between the namesakes is purely imaginary.

There are places in the Fens where level fields stretch to the circle of the horizon a few miles away, fields of potatoes, sugar beet, peas, brussels sprouts, cauliflowers, cabbages, for the land is extremely fertile. Many of the farms are large, so-called prairie farms, run very efficiently with the most modern equipment. Rarely a hedge anywhere in the Fens, even rarer a stone wall, for in all the fields there is hardly a stone. Even round the farms there are few clumps of trees, in the fields few rows of trees even for windbreaks.

Other places have smaller fields of daffodils and tulips. Here and there the sun glints on glasshouses. By the roadside are stalls selling flowers, vegetables, fruit and other produce. Near many a house, probably with a show of aubretias in Spring, there is an immensely tall mast for a television aerial.

Most of the land is arable but it is different from other arable districts. The hedgeless fields are divided by ditches, drains and dykes, straight as though ruled, gleaming like eelskin, tufted in places by bulrushes and reeds. At intervals the channels may be bridged by a huge drain pipe flanked by fat blue plastic bags full of earth or concrete to make it level for planks over which the farm traffic can pass. Some of the roads are as straight as the dykes, but others may have an unexpected sardonic twist like the plot of a short story.

On some of the roads you look at an embankment towering above you and see a boat passing along up there. The embankment is for a river, and the road is below the river bed—a result of land reclamation.

The Wash used to extend much farther inland than now. The old coastline can be traced by whorls of sea banks erected successively to keep out the high tides. Some of these banks, known as Rampers (from Ramparts) skirt the area known as Bicker Haven (where the Witham used to reach the sea), which did not silt up until early in Norman times. The villages—Anglo-Saxon for the most part—have been built in an arc round by Quadring, none of them on the Haven.

Material from the coast washed away by the sea has been deposited in the Wash, especially on the Lincolnshire shores. Fenland rivers flow sluggishly across the flat countryside and when they reach the sea they drop the silt they are carrying. Sea and rivers have built up a band of silt girdling the Wash, an area of drier, higher land on which settlements were established. Much of the silt area is called the Townlands for this reason.

Silting up continues. As more and more deposits are left, the level of the sea bed is raised. In time the shoreward fringe is exposed at low tide and salt marsh can form by the processes observed at Gibraltar Point and Rimac. A sea bank will keep the tides out, then the land can be reclaimed.

Back from the coast, things are slightly different. The Fens were not created by heavy rainfall. About 24 inches of rain fall in a year on Deeping Fen, for instance. What made the Fens was water settling on low flat land and spreading over it. Layers of peat were formed over an extensive area stretching in boomerang shape across the outer Fens.

Until it is drained, peatland cannot be worked. When it is drained, peat shrinks. Hence the road below the bed of the river. The rivers have to try to flow uphill on leaving the peat. Hence frequent flooding. When drained, peatland is fertile but it crumbles in dry weather, and is liable to blow away, taking newly planted seeds with it.

The fen dwellers had an unenviable reputation for lawlessness. True, they defied authority often enough and resorted to violence, but they were not political rebels. They acted in defence of their way of life, threatened as it was increasingly by drainage and enclosures. They bred horses (which were worked unshod, the soil was so soft), they fattened cattle, bred sheep, mowed fodder, cut osiers, sedge, reeds and turf, caught fish, took wildfowl and reared geese.

Life was difficult. Before reclamation, what good land was available tended to be overstocked, leading to cattle plague and other diseases. Where herds and flocks were built up, watch had to be kept for rustlers. Cattle had at times to swim to grazing and were brought back in boats; so with sheep, which were sometimes sheared in the boats. Despite the centuries of reclamation, floods continued. In 1799 hundreds of acres were harvested by men in boats or standing waist deep, cutting off the ears which appeared above the surface.

Malaria was prevalent. As a remedy the fen dwellers made up poppy juice into a paste and took a pellet of this opium the size of a pea. 'The effect on the taker and those about him is far less deleterious than excessive beer or dram drinking', was the opinion in 1895 of W. H. Wheeler, the Boston city engineer and excellent historian of the Fens. The opium habit continued well into this century. One explanation of the term 'yellow belly' for Lincolnshire people is that 'the ague' gave a yellowish tinge to the skin, especially under the clothing.

Ironically, in the swampy regions there was often a lack of good drinking water, the people depending on rain to fill pits which turned the water brackish if they were deep, and which, if shallow, soon dried up.

Attempts to reclaim fen land were made by religious houses in the Dark Ages. The Conqueror's chamberlain, Richard de Rulos, embanked the Welland and converted enough swamp into pasture for a settlement later known as Market Deeping (Deep Meadow). Peasants were successful in some districts at certain periods but the results were generally temporary.

As mentioned earlier, large-scale drainage operations were started at the end of Elizabeth I's reign.

Under Charles I, Dutch engineers were called in, among them Vermuyden, famous for his work in Axholme, and Sir Philibert Vernatti, who constructed the great Vernatt's Drain. Despite fierce opposition, efforts continued. Yet it was laborious to keep the channels open, and the peat shrank until the water on the land was below the level of the drainage channels supposed to carry it away.

To deal with this difficulty it was necessary to lift the water into the channels by mechanical means. From about 1760 a number of windmills were installed and their use increased for about a century. The mills worked large scoop wheels, as at Pode Hole, where the main drains of Deeping Fen converge. However, as the peat continued to shrink, the windmills were unable to cope. At last two splendidly constructed steam engines were brought to Pode Hole in 1825 and continued to work until 1928. Nearby another steam engine helped to drain Pinchbeck South Fen. It is possible to see what these engines are like if you go to the Blue Gowt Drain on Spalding Marsh in Pinchbeck, where the engine which worked from its installation in 1832 until 1952 has been preserved. As the peat went on shrinking, the scoop wheels of the engines had to be lowered in 1847 and five times more in the period until 1904. During World War II almost the whole of Deeping Fen was under the plough.

In the East and West Fens a supplementary approach was tried with considerable success about the beginning of the nineteenth century, when Rennie, Smeaton, Telford, Brunel and Robert Stephenson were among those called in for drainage schemes. New catchwater drains were cut, skirting the foot of high ground to prevent water from reaching the fens. Additional, internal drains were added, in conjunction with pumping stations.

These improvements and continued work on the rivers and drains have not yet done away with the risk of floods. In March 1947 the danger bell was tolled in Croyland Abbey for the first time since 1880. The Welland and Glen had overflowed and flooded twenty square miles, turning Croyland into an island again. British troops, aided by German prisoners of war, shared in controlling and restoring the situation.

The Rivals: Spalding and Croyland

One of the most remarkable sights in spring around Spalding is that of the village refuse tips, brilliant with thousands of tulip buds. They have been cut off so as to ripen the bulbs. Nevertheless not all the flowers are wasted. Between six and eight million tulip heads of different colours go to decorate the carnival floats for the May parade through Spalding, an event attended by thousands of visitors.

In the later 1880s some Spalding people began to collect snowdrop bulbs (sometimes employing gipsies) for medicinal purposes. One of them found he had more bulbs than he could dispose of and sent their flowers to London as an experiment. He went on to plant a few double daffodils and was pleasantly surprised by the demand. Soon he found that narcissus was the flower most called for. Disposal of the bulbs was then of secondary importance.

A new development dates from 1905 when the Darwin Tulip was introduced and rapidly found favour. After a set back during the First World War, with the industry restricted because it was not producing a food crop, there came a considerable expansion. Bulb growing gave many smallholders a higher return per acre. The forcing of bulbs started about 1920, when glass began to be erected on a small scale. Now glasshouses cover scores of acres and produce several hundred million tulips and daffodils each year. More daffodils and narcissi are grown in Britain than in any other country.

Despite the friendliness of the people, perhaps the thronged flower parade is not the best time to appreciate Spalding. An ordinary market day is preferable for wandering about the streets and along the banks of the Welland. Spalding has been called the most interesting town in Lincolnshire after Lincoln. It is customary to compare Spalding with somewhere in Holland. True, the channel of the tidal river is lined with trees, fine brick houses and warehouses. However, the houses above the grassy river banks are not gabled but have the nice façades typical of good building at the end of the eighteenth century and the beginning of the nineteenth.

The best way of getting to know Spalding is to go (on foot, of course) along the river bank, examining the buildings on your side and admiring those opposite. If you cross the High Bridge you can walk along to the bridge lower down (once the Chain Bridge) and retrace your steps on the other side. Near the High Bridge is the thatched White Horse inn, known as the George in coaching days. On the left bank is the market place, where the old Corn Exchange is being replaced by an Arts Centre; the long White Hart, another coaching inn, the Sheep Market and the Victorian Sessions House, built by Charles Kirk of Sleaford. Among the town houses, Willesby Hall stands out from its Georgian-type neighbours because it has early seventeenth-century gables and mullioned windows.

The right bank has the admirable Holland House of about 1760 near the big South Holland Mills built sixty years later with the use of rusticated cement, which is favoured in Spalding. On this side are two showpieces, the church and Ayscoughfee Hall. The church, cruciform, perhaps with a detached tower when it was built in 1284, has been made almost square by later additions. A slight cant to the east is attributed to its having been given no foundations at all. Inside, there is a striking number of arches, leading the eye up to the hammerbeam roof of the nave and its 28 wooden angels. An upper room of the north porch is reached by a winding stair. The large south chapel was used as a school in the nineteenth century.

Standing back from Church Gate, behind a long garden wall, is Ayscoughfee Hall, said to date from 1429 but modified according to eighteenth-century taste and again in 1845. Part of the house has been turned into a museum. The eighteenth-century gardens too have been modified to cater for modern visitors who enjoy lawns, flowers, yew hedges and lily pond.

The town bought Ayscoughfee Hall and grounds from the Johnson family as a memorial to the Jubilee of 1897, and the Urban District Council used to have its offices there. Ayscoughfee Hall was the home of the eighteenth-century lawyer Maurice Johnson, a friend of Linnaeus and a keen collector. He helped to found the Society of Antiquaries, of which he was the first Librarian. Before that, in 1710, Johnson started the Gentlemen's Society of Spalding. This was a social club, encouraging correspondence on literary and scientific subjects, and attracted many famous members, including Sir Isaac Newton, Sir Hans Sloane, Alexander Pope, Joseph Addison, the antiquarian William Stukeley, and the master of Spalding Grammar School, Richard Bentley, who went on to become Master of Trinity College, Cambridge. The Spalding Gentlemen's Society is still active, with its library and museum in Broad Street.

Spalding grew up around a Benedictine priory, of which little remains. For long the priory bedevilled relations with Croyland, its only rival. About 1052 Thorold of Buckenhale (said to have been Godiva's brother) seems to have founded Spalding Priory, which was regarded as a cell of Croyland. The trouble really started after the Conquest when, as already mentioned, Ivo Taillebois married Lucy, the heiress of Thorold, and settled at Spalding Castle (which stood east of the Pinchbeck Road but has now disappeared). The Norman Ivo became the fierce enemy of the Saxon abbey at Croyland and eventually succeeded in detaching Spalding Priory. The Priory's wealth and importance increased until it became, after Croyland, much the wealthiest foundation in Lincolnshire. In its heyday it entertained Edward I, Edward II, John of Gaunt and Geoffrey Chaucer.

The site of the Priory was near Spalding market place, and some fragments in a passage running south from the market place are traditionally associated with it. Opposite the end of the passage some old brick dwellings are believed to have been the dormitory. Then there is the Prior's Oven, an octagonal little stone building at the corner of the Sheep Market; it is claimed to be medieval. On the eastern edge of the town, Fulney Farm House is spoken of as the Priory dairy. Monk's Hall Farm, on the road to Bourne, is said to have been a grange of the Priory. Three miles outside Spalding are the ruins of Wykeham Chapel, roofless now but still with tracery in four of the great windows, built in 1311 by Prior Hatfield. If, as thought, it was the private chapel of the prior's country house, its original size and quality confirm the Priory's standing.

At Spalding the Welland crosses the stretch of silt between the freshwater fens and the salt marsh to seaward. The town developed as the lowest bridging point on the Welland until Fosdyke Bridge was opened in 1815. The river was navigable as far as Stamford, though Spalding High Bridge prevented tall sea-going vessels from passing farther upstream. Corn, flour, malt and stone came down the Welland from Stamford, and coal, groceries and timber were shipped in the opposite direction. Even after the railway reached Spalding in 1848 the Welland had to be maintained in good condition for flood prevention, thus ensuring that it remained navigable for smallish craft. This river trade was finally killed as motor traffic developed and now there is not even a rowing boat.

There are, however, many reminders of Spalding's history as a river port, fully described by Neil Wright in *Spalding: an industrial history,* published by the Lincolnshire Industrial Archaeology Group. There are, for instance, various mills and warehouses. Brewing was also important. The Albion Brewery (in two halves) fronting the Welland was built in 1824. Later the Brewery was used as a guano store, then as a chicory factory, in 1890 as a mineral water factory, and in 1934 one half became the central Fire Station, while the other half was taken over as a garage.

From the eighteenth century Spalding has been well known for its market 'gardiners' and nurserymen, 'asperigrass' of superior excellence and 'an apple called the Spalding rennet by the Gardiners'. Towards the end of last century it was noted that 'the growing of sugar beet has been tried in the fens but it grew too coarse and its cultivation was given up'. An alternative explanation you sometimes hear for the failure of the sugar beet is that at first the growers were ignorant of the rule 'One seed for the farmer, one for the skylark' (a real pest, for it may decimate a sowing). Other attempts were made but without much success until the Beet Sugar Subsidy Act was passed in 1925, after the danger of dependence on imported sugar had become apparent during the First World War. In 1926 the first sugar beet factory in Lincolnshire was built at Spalding, so sited that deliveries can be made without passing through the town.

On signposts to Spalding's old rival, and in postal addresses, the name is given as Crowland, but for the abbey it seems useful to retain the older form, Croyland. Cru-land, by the way, is soft and muddy land.

The abbey owes its founding to Guthlac, son of a Mercian nobleman, who gave up his military career, turned monk and decided in 699 to live as a hermit in the Lincolnshire Fens. He was brought by boat to a chosen spot on an island where a sow with a white litter lay under a willow tree—details which are reminiscent of the passage in Book VIII of Virgil's *Aeneid,* in which Father Tiber advised Aeneas on the site where Alba was to be founded. The Croyland site, Anchor Church Field, is about a mile from the ruins. A Mercian prince, Ethelbald, fleeing from his cousin and rival, came to Croyland and was assured by Guthlac that the kingship would be his. The prophecy came true and in gratitude Ethelbald founded the abbey in 716, two years after Guthlac's death.

The abbey was burned three times, once by the Danes about 850, when they murdered Abbot Theodore, whose skull is identified as the one still on view, and on another occasion by a careless plumber in 1091. It gave refuge to King Wilthaf, who was buried there in 825, and hospitality to Henry VI and Edward IV. Canute presented twelve polar bear skins to keep the priests' feet warm at the altar. Waltheof, Earl of Northumberland, gave Croyland the rich stone quarries of Barnack.

At the Dissolution, Henry VIII's commissioners pensioned the abbot off with £133 6s 8d for life, and demolished most of the buildings, leaving the north aisle to continue as the parish church —as it still does. During the Civil War Crowland was Royalist. A force raided Spalding, took hostages, including the Puritan vicar, and exposed them on defensive earthworks at Crowland to discourage artillery reprisals. After being fortified, the abbey was later bombarded by Cromwell in 1643. Neglect, even more damaging, followed until in the nineteenth century devout restorations began.

The surviving west front is rich in statues, several tiers of them, of saints, apostles, kings and abbots, once totalling 29. The old west door of the nave has a quatrefoil showing scenes from Guthlac's life. Through this doorway there is a view of a Norman arch, comparable in interest and poignant in its isolation. It is worth walking down to examine it from different angles and also to look at the stone screen under it, marked by a fire which in 1796 roasted a bullock at the coming of age of the lord of the manor's eldest son.

In Crowland village, a prosperous community, the streets are unusually wide, retaining trees planted in the eighteenth century. At the meeting of the four main streets is Crowland's unique triangular bridge. The streams that once flowed under its three arches have long since been covered in. A charter of 942 refers to a triangular bridge here but the present structure dates from John of Gaunt's time, even if it is not now believed that he built it. On one of the three flights of steps is a seated figure, vehemently denied to represent Oliver Cromwell with a bun, as the facetious have suggested. One authority identifies the figure as that of the Virgin, others as Christ, crowned, holding the orb. Some add that the statue came from the western gable of the church, taken down in 1720. Men used to come to the bridge to be hired by the day, and the town crier rang his bell from the summit.

Island and Townland

The band or island of silt which the Welland crosses at Spalding lifts the main road a foot or two above the level of the fen as it leads eastwards. As will soon be apparent, it is a fascinating highway in its own right, and it is the key to a maze of smaller roads, some very small indeed. These side roads turn and twist among the dykes, where an alert eye may catch sight of a coypu escaped from Norfolk, or where a half-tame cock pheasant may try in vain to outstare a half-wild black and white duck across a ditch. Other roads balance on the top of ridges which are old sea banks, now several miles inland, and eventually at the shore when the tide is up there may be cows grazing on one side and round-eyed seals on the other.

Every mile or two along the main road on Holbeach 'island' there is a village. Each has a magnificent church: Weston, Moulton,

Whaplode, Holbeach, Gedney and Long Sutton, to mention the best known. They do not form a group but one thing they have in common is the mystery of how they came to be built on such a scale in a region without stone. No doubt ecclesiastical rivalry had something to do with it, for Spalding built Moulton, while Croyland built Whaplode and Gedney. The churches are mentioned here in order from east to west and carefully not ranked according to supposed merit. Each of them is famous for many excellences.

South of the main road the villages have their stretches of Fen; north of it, their Marsh; some also have their Drove, originally an uncultivated strip. Dodging about, as though exasperated by the tangle of drains, there is a very crooked road called Roman.

Holbeach parish is said to comprise 21,000 acres of land and 14,000 acres of water. The de Multon family were lords of the manor and obtained a charter for a market and fair in 1252. John de Kirton, of the family which took over, founded a hospital in 1351 on a site now occupied by the Chequers Inn. A Holbeach man became bishop of Lincoln in 1547 and took as his family name the name of the town, though he had been born Henry Rands. Bishop Holbeach is not a general favourite, for he enriched himself by giving up the estates of the see to the Crown.

A more popular citizen is the antiquarian William Stukeley, even if his father did pull down the ruins of John de Kirton's hospital. Born in 1687, Stukeley practised medicine in Boston and Grantham. He helped to found the Society of Antiquaries in London and was its Secretary for the first nine years; he joined the Spalding Gentlemen's Society in 1722. A friend of Newton, Stukeley was an enthusiastic believer in the influence of the Druids. In 1727 he took holy orders and did well for himself, being at the same time Vicar of All Saints in Stamford and Rector of Somerby near Grantham. He retired from both livings in 1748 and spent the rest of his days until 1765 in London. On one occasion he postponed a service at Stamford so that the congregation could watch an eclipse of the sun. When 75 years old he took as his text 'Now we see through a glass darkly' for the first sermon he preached wearing spectacles.

From Holbeach you can zigzag along the lanes, between the fields, past grazing cattle and sheep and parading pheasants, past field gates and sluice gates, by side drains, startling a heron or some mallard, screamed at by gulls, dive-bombed by lapwings, in time finding the way blocked by an earthen rampart, the final sea bank. But its slope can be mounted and on top there is a track for miles above the flat, flat shore. There are miles of marsh, at first glimpse rather drab but soon revealing unexpectedly varied tones of dun, amber, ochre, mackerel, woad. Bird watchers erect a hide at a favourite spot, a few campers put up brightly coloured tents, some hardy souls may use an old boat as a picnic hut, and do it often enough to put up an aerial. All who venture on the marsh should beware of treacherous channels and especially of incoming tides.

Last century it was suggested that a whole new county could be formed by marshland reclaimed from the Wash. The plan fell through but there have been successful reclamations, including one of 1,500 acres north of Holbeach Hurn in 1948. Such land is surprisingly soon available for grazing, and subsequently it is drained in readiness for cultivation.

In this part of Lincolnshire, as near Caistor, farmers grow peas and other vegetables on contract to fulfill the demand by the pre-packing trade. The percentage of high quality grades has been much increased within the existing acreage, thanks to improvements in varieties and techniques. For such enterprises, large farms are the rule.

On the smallholdings, as well as flower bulbs, tomatoes are grown in glasshouses, as are millions of cauliflower plants to be planted out in the fields. All are pricked out individually and about half the number are actually grown on in pots for this purpose. In addition, several million cabbage and brussels sprout plants are raised under glass annually.

A drovers' road for moving cattle to the markets at King's Lynn and Norwich passed through the parish of Long Sutton. It led over Cross Keys Wash, regarded with justice as highly dangerous. Guides on horseback used to pilot vehicles and people across at low tide, the foot passengers riding pillion behind the guides. Perhaps, much earlier, King John had taken advantage of this service, but his baggage and treasure took another route and were lost 'in the Wash', as every schoolchild knows. A couple of miles north of the main road, King John's Farm is supposed to be the site of a house where he stayed the night after the disaster. Many people have searched in vain for his treasure.

Sutton Bridge, a very long village, has a great hydraulic swing bridge across the river Nene—which could, but does not, form the county boundary on the east. Before the present bridge there was a swing bridge by Robert Stephenson, which in 1850 replaced a wooden bridge by Rennie and Telford. These last two men came on the scene at the time when the river was canalised for some miles to its mouth. Further improvements encouraged a railway scheme for a port at Sutton Bridge, and in 1881 new docks were opened. Only a month later the port scheme had been abandoned, for by then the docks had already collapsed. Today at the mouth of the Nene, a pleasant place, there are two lighthouses, one of them occupied for a while by Peter Scott.

It is from Sutton Bridge that hunters have set out to shoot baby seals in the Wash, as licensed by the Home Office, in a controversial enterprise. In 1973 the pelts for coats and handbags fetched £10 each. About 380 animals were involved that year.

All but lost among the fen byways, in a dingle at Tydd St Mary, the villagers have established the tiniest nature reserve I have seen. Reeds and rushes hide mallard and teal, there are bird boxes for rare visitors like goldfinches and for more regular visitors, and occasionally geese, snipe and curlew visit it. Just above the reserve is a village sign, showing the most famous person associated with Tydd St Mary, a one-time rector, Nicholas Brakespear, the only English pope (Adrian IV, 1154-59). Strawberries grow in the middle of this delightful hamlet. Near them a modernised cottage still has its very thick seventeenth-century walls, and in an outhouse, now a garage, a sawyer's pit. The owner remembered destroying magpies' eggs for farmers as a lad, complained about the plagues of pheasants and, worse, of hares which systematically go along the rows of sugar beet and cauliflowers, wished for more foxes to keep them down, and spoke knowledgeably about English and French partridges.

The churches around Holbeach are remarkable in themselves and because of their concentration. Between Spalding and Boston there are more churches of note, not all close together but none the less outstanding. Some of them are mentioned in a rhyme:

Gosberton church is very high
Surfleet church is all awry
Pinchbeck church is in a hole
And Spalding church is fit to foal.

The list is generally regarded as inadequate as well as unflattering. It is an unfortunate fact that on the way to Boston and also on the Townland silt area, there are far too many churches, and the villages they grace, to be mentioned here.

Gilbert White of Selbourne wrote: 'Lands that are subject to frequent inundations are always poor; and probably the reason may be because the worms are drowned'. Fen worms seem able to survive, for the Fens are anything but poor, as we have seen. However, certain crops have been abandoned, such as flax, hemp, chicory and woad.

Long Sutton, Skirbeck (until 1938) and Boston are among the places which have experimented with woad, a pretty yellow flower in the border, incidentally. When hunting for the abandoned woad mill at Algarkirk, I was reduced to asking its whereabouts at a farm; of course it turned out to be opposite the car among the farm buildings. The Latin name for woad is *Isatis tinctoria*, and a colony named Isatica was founded in the eighteenth century for woad growing on the North Forty Foot Drain near Brothertoft.

Brothertoft used to be known as Goosetoft, for reasons indicated in 1640 by John Taylor, the Water Poet (who must have found a home from home in the Fens):

The people here have neither horse nor cowe,
Nor sheep, nor oxe, nor asses, pig, nor sowe;
Nor cream, curds, whey, buttermilk or cheese,
Nor any other living thing but geese.

Geese were reared for the London market, to which they walked after having been driven across a patch of hot tar to toughen their feet. Others were kept for meat and eggs, but their most important products in the Fens were feathers and quills. There were five pluckings a year, sometimes done barbarously. Enclosures reduced the trade in feathers, as the popularity of Birmingham's steel nibs reduced the demand for quill pens. There were, however, two factories for purifying and preparing goose feathers at Boston at the end of last century. Whether the geese provided fertiliser is not mentioned, but fish manure was certainly used. Sticklebacks from the Fens and the Witham, sprats from the Wash and sometimes mussels went to feed the land.

St Botolph's Town

Most of the historic Boston lies on the left bank of the Witham, between a windmill on the north and a ruined brick tower to the south, clustering round three bridges across the river. Nearly all the interesting sights are within a few minutes' walk of the Town Bridge, the middle one, which leads from the right bank of the Witham to the capacious market place, with medieval alleyways opening off it.

The Witham is tidal as far as Boston, and only at the town is it narrow enough to be bridged. Boston is not recorded in the Domesday survey. A church dedicated to St Botolph existed, however, in the township of Skirbeck, now a southern suburb of Boston. St Botolph, a white-haired Benedictine monk, revered by the Danes despite being Anglo-Saxon, may never have been in Lincolnshire, but his cult was widespread, helped by taking wonder-working parts of his corpse to various abbeys. More than seventy churches in England were dedicated to him. Around his church by the Witham a settlement grew up, known as St Botolph's town until Tudor times, after which the name Boston came to be preferred.

The lowest of the three bridges is Haven Bridge. Almost opposite its eastern end is Boston Grammar School. In the old school yard is a brick building, now the library, but dating from Mary Tudor's time, when it was the 'Big School', replacing an old one in the lane called Wormgate (a corruption of Witham Gate) near the great church. The 'Big School' was built on the old Mart Yard. About 1200 the market was transformed into St Botolph's Fair, so important that within a generation the Court of Hustings in London suspended its sittings in order that merchants could go to Boston.

English monasteries kept representatives in the town to lay in supplies of wine, groceries and cloth. Traders from Flanders, Germany, Italy and Scandinavia came to exchange their wares for English products, including hides and salt. Wine was imported from Gascony in large quantities, and perhaps from the Rhine, for there was an inn of the Three Kings in Dauphin Lane off the Market Place, the three kings being the Magi, who are supposed to be buried at Cologne. The three crowns of the Boston coat of arms are sometimes said to be theirs. By 1270 the port of Boston was pre-eminent in England, and in 1289 Boston paid more in customs duties than London.

St Botolph's church in Boston was built during the prosperous times. Work on it began in 1309, when a pit more than thirty feet deep was dug and, it is said, quantities of raw wool were thrown into it to make sure foundations. Most of the building was done under Edward II and Edward III but the superlative tower was not finished until 1460.

The Stump, as the tower is popularly known, tops 272 feet, in three stages, past buttresses and huge windows to the elaborate parapet, pinnacles and flying buttresses where the octagonal lantern begins, and on to the topmost parapet and final pinnacles. On the south side of the tower is a statue most people agree represents St Botolph. On the tower's west front are dated flood marks—1781, for example, 1807, 1810 . . . and 21st January 1953, when a fish was swept into the aisles. The wind eddies round the tower, as many a bride has regretted when her veil is blown awry, sometimes clean away.

The Stump compels admiration so effortlessly that the height of the church is generally assumed to be its unusual dimension. It is very long too, as a matter of fact, 282 feet. The length can be appreciated from the churchyard. If you look at the churchyard, you see that it slopes upwards from the Witham because the rich were buried near the river, the poor farther away, and as the poor were more numerous, the ground has been built up.

If possible, the inside of the church should be visited when lighted by the setting sun through the great west window; but under any conditions the interior is magnificent. The tower goes up, open, nearly 140 feet. The weight of the tower is pushing the church away, and pillars in the north aisle are clearly out of true. Up in the roof the bosses are carved with subjects from Boston's history, an extraordinary collection worth hours of study.

In 1803, according to a notice, the roof timber was damaged by a fire started by a plumber using a grate without a pan underneath. Perhaps that is why the chapel opening off the west end was turned into an 'engine house' for the fire engine. Later, part of it was used as a Blue Coat School but it is, of course, now the Cotton Chapel, named after the famous Puritan vicar who went to North America. The decision to give the chapel this name was Herbert Ingram's, a Boston man who founded the *Illustrated London News* in 1842 and became patron of the living. Ingram also provided a water supply for the town, for which he was MP, and is himself commemorated by a statue erected in the market place after he and his son had been drowned in Lake Michigan in 1860. American visitors had expressed surprise that there was no memorial to John Cotton in the church, and the vicar, Canon Blenkin, and Pishey Thompson, the local historian, who had lived in the States, approached Edward Everett, married to one of Cotton's descendants, for help in restoring the old south-west chapel. Everett's appeal met with a generous response and in 1857 the American Ambassador was present at a thanksgiving service. Boston in Massachusetts has more than once aided its Lincolnshire namesake.

England has few, if any, finer choir stalls than those at Boston. All but two out of 64 have their misericords. They are carved on the underside in a series which rivals Lincoln's. The elbow rests and poppy-heads are also decorated. Many subjects are grotesque or satirical; some represent everyday medieval life, from bear baiting to a beggar soliciting alms. All these were carved about 1390, and they inspired good craftsmanship by the Victorians who added the canopies.

Among the monuments are an alabaster knight and an alabaster lady. In 1340 a Hanseatic merchant named Wissel Smalenburg from Münster died in Boston and his portrait was incised on a six-foot slab of black Tournai marble, which was found near the Grammar

School on the site of the 'Grey Friars' church and brought here. Nearly fifty years later, the Boston merchant Walter Pescod and his wife were commemorated by a brass detailed enough to show the pea pods which gave him his name.

The Boston coat of arms is represented, including three crowns, a well-developed mermaid on each side, and a ram on a woolsack above them all. The mermaids are a reminder that in 1573 the Mayor acquired the title of Admiral of the Wash, when a Court of Admiralty was established for Boston Corporation. Pirates in the Wash were attacking ships at that period.

The beginning of the end of the old order, in which church, guilds and king were supreme, came in 1536, when there were disturbances in and around Boston, as at Louth and other places. Subsequent changes are illustrated in the careers of three men. First, John Taverner, the great Boston musician, once a privileged member of Cardinal Wolsey's circle, repented of his 'songs to Popish ditties', turned reformer and acted as Thomas Cromwell's agent in Boston. Second, in 1517 John Foxe was born on a site in Boston market place where the Rum Puncheon inn now stands. Foxe's *History of the Acts and Monuments of the Church* (the *Book of Martyrs*), with its stories of persecuted Protestants, was influential in shaping the religious and social spirit which flowered as Puritanism.

The third man was John Cotton, vicar of St Botolph's from 1612 to 1633. He was a fervent Puritan, and active politically. The basis of his power was Boston's wealth as a market for produce from the Fens, which enabled the town Corporation to act with defiant independence in appointing (and paying) Puritan clergy. While Cotton was vicar, Boston men refused to pay a forced loan in 1627, among other examples of insubordination. Cotton encouraged membership of the Massachusetts Bay Company and supported its schemes for a colony in America. He did much to inspire the remarkable group of stern, principled Lincolnshire men who played such a part in founding and developing Boston in Massachusetts. The Puritan movement centred on Boston in Lincolnshire provided many settlers in America, some of them prominent. Five men from old Boston were elected governors of Massachusetts, and eight were among the founders or early overseers of Harvard. Times had indeed changed from 1607, when (as mentioned) Separatists from Gainsborough were arrested and tried in Boston for seeking religious liberty overseas. Only when his enemy, Laud, became Archbishop of Canterbury in 1633 was Cotton forced to leave Boston. From Sempringham, then a Puritan stronghold, he managed to join a ship sailing for Massachusetts. There he aided those who built up the new settlement with the old name.

When the Civil War broke out, Boston was, of course, within the sphere of influence of the Eastern Association and supported Parliament. One of Boston's two MPs, Sir Anthony Irby, arrested the Royalist Sir Edward Heron of Gosberton, High Sheriff of Lincolnshire, and aided by Cromwell, captured Crowland from the King's troops. As Parliamentary forces began to build up for an offensive, some of the soldiery bivouacked in St Botolph's. Several officers in the Lincolnshire Regiment of the New Model Foot commanded by the radical Thomas Rainborowe (or Rainsborough) were emigrants to New England who had come back to fight against the king. Among them was a captain, John Leverett, who returned to Massachusetts and became its governor in 1673.

In the seventeenth century Boston shaped the course of events in America. During the eighteenth century Boston shaped the history of Australia.

Leaving aside for the time being the part played in this by Sir Joseph Banks of Revesby, Recorder of Boston from 1809 to 1820, a major rôle fell to George Bass. He was born in 1771 at Aswarby, as noted, but while a child came with his widowed mother to Skirbeck, where the family kept an inn. Bass was a boyhood friend of Matthew Flinders from Donington, and together they explored the Australian coast and sailed round Tasmania. It was Bass who discovered the strait between Australia and Tasmania which bears his name, and he made many other discoveries. Bass ended badly, however. After a series of setbacks, he disappeared on a trading voyage in 1803 and much later was rumoured to have been seen working as a prisoner in a South American copper mine.

Flinders ended sadly after a brilliant career. Following his explorations with Bass, he sailed round Australia and, among other things, surveyed the Great Barrier Reef. As he went, he gave

Lincolnshire names to many places, and others have been given his name, among them the Flinders Range. On trying to return to England in 1803 he survived shipwreck, only to be held for seven years by the French on Mauritius. His health was shattered, and he died at Donington, where he had aroused little interest, in 1814. Next day his important book, *A Voyage to Terra Australis,* was published. Flinders's daughter became Mrs Petrie, and her son was Sir Flinders Petrie, the archaeologist.

In the eighteenth century a big stimulus to Boston's development came with expansion east and then west of the town, following improved drainage. Then there was the opening of the Grand Sluice in 1766 to regulate the tides and prevent silting. The massive lock system and the accompanying bridges for foot and wheeled traffic are still sights to admire, somewhat north of the Stump. Hopes were not altogether realised, though a visitor to the official opening of the Grand Sluice, disappointed perhaps by the hospitality, may have been too bitter:

Boston, Boston, thou hast nought to boast on
But a Grand Sluice and a high steeple,
A proud, conceited, ignorant people,
And a coast where souls get lost on.

As shown by the new warehouses that were built just south of the market place, the port revived, with larger ships enabled to use it. An early anticipation of the better times had been the building of the elegant Custom House in 1725, well timed to cope with the growth of smuggling, which reached such an extent by 1823 that it needed four waggons to bring contraband from a ship off Wrangle to the excisemen. Rennie designed an iron bridge in 1806 where the present Town Bridge (1913) stands, and he banked the flood wall there. The Corporation Building had been put up on one side of the old wooden bridge in 1722; it replaced the Guildhall as Town Hall, being replaced in turn by the Municipal Buildings in 1904. Just to the south there are some fine warehouses (once there were more), which cry out for conservation, but they stand just where road widening would be advantagous from a traffic planner's point of view. In 1822 the Assembly Rooms were opened on the other side of Rennie's bridge. The fish market there can easily be located by its appeal to the senses.

As usual the railways, which came in 1848, diverted traffic from the port for a time, and trade fell off by more than a half. Then in the 1880s maritime traffic revived, following an outlay of £160,169 0s 9d on new docks. You walk there past the Haven Bridge, past an extraordinary split house built in two halves connected only by a brick crossbar from which nets used to be hung to dry. The path follows a river curve, giving picturesque views (mainly rear views, unlike Spalding) across the Witham. Ships up to 3,000 tons can use Boston docks, which are as endlessly fascinating to a visitor as docks everywhere. Timber imports, a feature of the medieval trade, are continued in our day by Soviet ships.

Diagonally across from the Stump a much restored timber-framed building marks an especially interesting neighbourhood. The building is Shodfriars' Hall, named after the Black Friars or Dominicans, in 1222 the first Order of friars to be attracted to Boston by its rapid growth. A few yards farther on is a house surmounted by a stone dog, the Dominican symbol (*domini canis*), baring its teeth at Packhorse Quay. Just beyond the Custom House is Spain Lane, named after the family of William de Spayne, a rich merchant of the Corpus Christi guild and sheriff of Lincolnshire in 1378. Most of the huge wine cellars which used to exist in Spain Lane, some rented by various abbeys to store wine from Bordeaux were destroyed in 1590. Part of the Dominican Friary was in Spain Lane. Some of the southern range of the cloisters still exists. It is renowned today as Blackfriars Hall.

Blackfriars was acquired in 1935 by the Boston Preservation Trust, and a Blackfriars Trust was formed in 1961. The ground floor seems to have been used as a warehouse, the upper floor (once thought to have been the refectory) is believed to have contained a series of study cells. When the Puritans were forbidden to attend the parish church after the Restoration they worshipped in Blackfriars, but after they could build chapels it became a warehouse. In our days the efforts of the Blackfriars Trust have transformed Blackfriars into an arts centre, complete with theatre—a notable achievement with happy consequences for a wide area around Boston.

The Boston Preservation Trust has also acquired other property in the area but the immediate purpose on its foundation in 1935 was to save Fydell House, next to the Guildhall, from demolition by property developers. Fydell House, built in 1726 for William Fydell, a wine merchant who was an Alderman and three times Mayor of Boston, has fortunately been preserved despite damage to the roof and top floor by German incendiary bombs on Good Friday, 1941. Behind the wrought-iron screen of the forecourt is an elaborate doorway. Carved and panelled oak and pine and Rococo plasterwork distinguish the interior, where the staircase is especially fine. Since 1946 the house has been occupied by Pilgrim College, an extra-mural department of Nottingham University, but local societies are permitted and encouraged to meet there.

Next door, overlooking the garden of Fydell House, is the Guildhall. Originally the hall of the Guild of St Mary, this brick building has a great window on the first floor looking across the street to the river. The new Corporation took it over as a town hall in 1546 and it was used for municipal purposes until this century. On the ground floor are the kitchens, which still have two ingenious spits driven by fans operated by hot air in the chimney flue.

A spiral staircase led up to the Court Room from the cells where Brewster, Bradford and others of the Pilgrim Fathers awaited trial in 1607. On the first floor are the Banqueting Hall (part of the Court Room) with the big west window and a gallery. The former Court Room, now a museum, displays items devoted to the woad industry, local bank notes (some issued by Jean Ingelow's father), fire marks and other items. Beyond is the Council Chamber, containing a splendid fifteenth-century linenfold panelled cupboard. The rooms on the first floor have other exhibits and some fine pictures, including portraits of Sir Joseph Banks and others.

Boston deserves warm congratulations not only on conserving these outstanding buildings, but for finding appropriate uses for them. It would be fitting if the warehouses opposite the Guildhall could also be acquired, perhaps as a Maritime Museum which could prove of more than local importance.

And so at last to the ruined Hussey Tower which is the southern limit of the Boston we have been concerned with. It is near the

Grammar School playing fields. Three unsteady floors of a square brick tower, with a stair turret and crenellated parapets, have been left despite demolitions since 1565. Approached by a field path among weeds and nettles and brambles, the tower is part of the home of Lord Hussey executed in 1536.

There is another tower, rather similar, the Rochford Tower, in Fishtoft. On the walls of a first floor room are indications of mural paintings. This tower is sometimes referred to as the Kyme Tower. It may have been built early in the sixteenth century, when the property belonged to the abbots of Westminster and was held by the Rochford family. Sir John de Rochford's daughter Margaret married Sir Frederick Tilney of Boston and is reputed to have laid the foundation stone of St Botolph's church in 1309.

At the other end of Boston, where the roads fork for Horncastle or for Spilsby and Skegness, is the Maud Foster windmill, with five sails and ogee cap. It was built in 1809 by the Reckitt brothers, Thomas and Isaac. Maud Foster was perhaps the owner of the land through which the Maud Foster Drain was cut in 1568. Corn came by barge along the Drain to the mill. An iron footbridge from 1811 is Telford's work.

The Fens north of Boston

On a clear day Boston Stump and Lincoln cathedral are just within sight of each other, although thirty miles apart. There are fens within a few miles of Lincoln. They are a southerly continuation of the lowlands stretching down from the Ancholme valley. Fen and lowland merge in a strange region of streams and drains and lanes and remnants of once deep woods. Few medieval villages were established there but several religious houses were—Bardney, Barlings, Stainfield, Stixwould, Tupholme. None survives. Nor, following the Witham south, does Kirkstead, though fortunately we do have its lovely and interesting tiny chapel of St Leonard.

Coal mining does not seem to go naturally with the development of a spa, but at Woodhall Spa the failure of the one led to the success of the other. The mining was associated with ambitions to plant a new forest and found a new city at the beginning of last century. All three were carried out by John Parkinson, who in 1802 was appointed steward to Sir Joseph Banks. Just east of Woodhall, not then a spa, Parkinson planted fir and oak which eventually grew into a sizeable forest. In 1811 he started boring for coal on the Woodhall estate of the Hotchkin family. At 540 feet the shaft was flooded with clear, salt water, but the work went on. Reports of success aroused considerable excitement, the bells of Horncastle church being rung one night to announce that coal had been found. The reports were based on samples of coal brought up by the workmen. Too late Parkinson found that the samples had been previously smuggled into the shaft. At last he had to abandon his project. In 1827 he went bankrupt. His forest was bought by his agent, Ostler, and became known as Ostler's Plantation, now much reduced. We shall come to Parkinson's city of New Bolingbroke presently. He is said to have ended as a turnkey in Lincoln jail.

The salty water which had invaded the mine was soon discovered to help sufferers from gout and rheumatism. Its reputation spread and Woodhall Spa now has modern baths, very pleasantly situated in a clearing in a considerable pinewood. The little town grew up on a sandy heath where the roads are lined with pines, birch, heather and bracken. Waterloo Wood, of oak, was planted soon after the battle, as noted on a column set up by its founder, Colonel Elmhirst, in 1844. Near the famous golf links is the brick Tower on the Moor, a fifteenth-century work attributed to the Cromwell family at Tattershall. During the Second World War, Woodhall was the base for 617 Squadron of the RAF, famous as the Dam Busters.

A few miles from its confluence with the Witham, the Bain flows through Coningsby. The clock on the church tower has an enormous dial and only the hour hand, but that is so big you can tell the time to within a minute or so. Such clocks are now very uncommon, and Coningsby folk hold that theirs is unique, the biggest of its kind in the world. On the road to the Fens is Lea Gate Inn, said to be on the site of the last of the old Guide Houses. Old irons, from which a torch was hung to direct travellers, are still in place.

On the Bain and adjoining Coningsby is Tattershall, with one of Lincolnshire's greatest buildings, the lowering brick keep of

Tattershall Castle. In size and strength it recalls a fortress but the interior suggests a palace. It was built about 1445 for Ralph Cromwell, Treasurer of England (his emblem a purse). The bricks were thought to be from Flanders but it is now known that 322,000 were hand-made for the job at Edlington Moor, a few miles away. Some are redder than average, some greyer, and those on the roof tend to be bright pink. From the roof, more than 100 feet up, there is a wide panorama, including Lincoln and Boston. The architect has not been identified. The story that he was Bishop Waynflete is dismissed as ridiculous in the official Guide.

Ralph, 3rd Baron Cromwell, rebuilt an earlier castle at Tattershall, built the church and a college (vanished), re-endowed almshouses. He died without heirs, and his properties had sundry owners before going to the Fortescues of Devon. For two centuries the castle was left to become derelict, which it did on an appropriate scale. In 1910 the Fortescue estates were sold. Lord Curzon intervened to circumvent an American buyer, and thus saved the Keep, its magnificent fireplaces and other features. After an enormous reconstruction, Curzon bequeathed Tattershall to the National Trust.

Like the Keep, Tattershall church is big but unlike it, is built of Ancaster stone. Most of the old glass has gone—illegally given by Lord Fortescue in 1757 to the Earl of Exeter for St Martin's Church, Stamford, and for Burghley House. Tattershall brasses in the church are famous. It is unusual to find so many, and such fine late ones, in a Lincolnshire church. Legend has it that Tom Thumb is buried in Tattershall church, and his house (a model of suitable size) is pointed out on a cottage in the market place.

The Bain joins the Witham at Dogdyke. The whole stretch of the Witham from Lincoln to Boston provides some of the best coarse angling in England, and Dogdyke is a good centre. At the Packet Inn there is a stretch of water owned by the Lincolnshire River Authority, which permits fishing by holders of a rod licence along 250 miles of bank in the county. The Authority does much work in fishery management. It battles with the problems of weeds, encouraged by fertilisers, and of pollution, and also the reduction of the biological oxygen content caused by sugars and carbohydrates released into the water by vegetable-washing plants. So as to prevent winter flooding in some areas, the water level has to be kept very low. While this has the beneficial side effect of reducing weeds, it leads to difficulties for fish, especially the fry and very small fish.

Contenders in fishing matches arranged by the Witham Joint Angling Committee try not to think of Sir Joseph Banks's procedures and results. In 1778 he organised one of his fishing parties by tented barge from Dogdyke to Boston, attended by a band. The party of 25 caught 32 pounds of pike and perch, 18 pounds of salmon and half a pound of flounders, which were cooked in the kitchen of Fydell House.

The road Sir Joseph used to take from Boston to his seat at Revesby goes by the silt and gravel spine through Stickney and Stickford. We can go by a more attractive road, possible since the East and West Fens were drained, partly through Banks's efforts. The way passes the green umbrellas sheltering anglers along the Maud Foster Drain, past the aqueduct taking catchwater over fen water in the Maud Foster, past the disused chimney (at the foot of a rainbow when I last saw it) marking the electrified Lade Bank pumping station, with a view of Sibsey's six-sailed trader windmill. When winter is dying, the grassy bank beside the roadside drain is quite hoary with snowdrops on the section known as the Seven Mile Straight.

Presently we come to a strange and interesting little place, New Bolingbroke, the 'city' founded by John Parkinson, of whom we heard at Woodhall Spa. Parcels of newly drained fen were allotted to existing parishes. In this way the village of Bolingbroke acquired land, in which Parkinson bought shares. He built a factory in 1824, with a crescent of terraced houses for the work-people. The crescent is an unusual sight in such a district, even if the impression is modified by the presence of a petrol pump as centrepiece. Parkinson had plans for a transport drain to New Bolingbroke through Boston, but as we have seen, fate was against him.

In the fens your eye becomes accustomed to a horizon which is little more than a line, almost abstract. It comes as a surprise when from the Seven Mile Straight the horizon shows up as a thick brush mark, a sign that the Wolds lie beyond. Revesby is at the foot of the Wolds.

The Revesby estate and sixty farms came to the Banks family in 1714. There had been an abbey there, founded in 1142, which had vanished by then. Sir Joseph lived in a Revesby Abbey, built on the site of the abbot's house. The present house is not Banks's but a nineteenth-century replacement.

Born in 1743, Banks became one in a great series of naturalist explorers. From 1768 to 1771 he accompanied Captain Cook to the Pacific in the *Endeavour.* This voyage started the passionate advocacy which led him to be called the Father of Australia. He was interested in founding new settlements to make up for losses in America. He had a hand in starting the great wool industry in the southern hemisphere by secretly obtaining some merino sheep from Spain for Australia and South Africa. He obtained vine cuttings for South Africa. He encouraged the use of citrus fruit against scurvy. He sent Captain Bligh in the *Bounty* to take breadfruit from Tahiti to the West Indies. That was after he had become scientific adviser at Kew.

In Lincolnshire, Banks was active in draining the fens, an effort not always appreciated, for it stirred up riots in Boston that needed the Scots Guards to quell them. In a difficult period for Boston, he imported quantities of rice, which he distributed together with recipes for cooking this unfamiliar food. Banks was enthusiastic about enclosures and better methods of agriculture, and he was the greatest planter of trees in Lincolnshire until the Yarboroughs of Brocklesby. He commissioned Nattes and others to draw Lincolnshire buildings for posterity. He was a keen amateur archaeologist. All this is the briefest indication of Sir Joseph Banks's activities.

He was a big man, over seventeen stone, as we know from his passion for weighing people, including visitors as well as his wife and his eccentric sister, who used wool from his sheep for the three dresses she wore turn and turn about, called Hightum, Titum and Scrub in descending order of favour.

'The Aviary of England'

As you go from Boston to the sea shore you are quite likely to see a heron reluctantly struggling into the air from a very narrow ditch. Gilbert White was his usual observant self in commenting that herons 'seem encumbered with too much sail for their light bodies; but these vast hollow wings are necessary in carrying burdens, such as large fishes, and the like'.

Below Boston, the tidal canalised stretch of the Witham known as the Haven passes through cauliflower fields (and historic places) to the Wash. Pilots are necessary to bring ships up the river to Boston Dock. At the Scotia Creek sea bank beyond Fishtoft a simple shaft on a square base commemorates the first attempt of those later known as the Pilgrim Fathers to find religious freedom across the seas in 1607.

Some Frieslanders are supposed to have founded Freiston. Enthusiasm for sea bathing late in the eighteenth century led to the development of Freiston Shore, which became a fashionable resort. The sea has retreated since then but on the marsh there are many flowers, some uncommon, among the sea grass. High tides give the shore the appearance of a lagoon, very beautiful at sunset and even more so just after dawn. Away in the fields is a striking white house with two Dutch-style stepped gables, one dated 1614. The first white loaf of bread to be baked in England is said to have been made here, and the house is naturally known as White Loaf Hall.

Freiston is the first of yet another succession of lovely churches which are to be found between Boston and Wainfleet. Only one or two of the villages are on the main road; the others have grown up on the marsh behind a succession of sea banks, including the so-called Roman Bank, of disputed date.

Wainfleet is sometimes under-rated as a town, but the large market place still suggests the bustle of long-past stock sales, and some of the side-streets have an atmosphere of more leisurely days. The Witham used to reach the sea near Wainfleet, which was a port for long after the Romans built it up, as Vannona, into their principal harbour on this coast. The sea is now several miles away.

In 1457 the town obtained a charter through William of Waynflete, Bishop of Winchester, first Provost of Eton, Lord Chancellor to Henry VI and founder of Magdalen College, Oxford. In 1484 he founded Magdalen College School in Wainfleet, the town's most famous building. The school is two storeys high, built of small red bricks, its entrance flanked by two burly polygonal towers. It must be added that Wainfleet School—now a secondary modern—is surrounded by recent, essential but totally dissimilar school buildings.

We have overshot Friskney, a village on the Fens side of the main road, among a web of lanes, with the big Catchwater Drain to the west. The merits of Friskney church are well known—its woodwork, for instance, ranks with that of the great Marshland churches. Medieval wall paintings, now much faded, were discovered during restoration in 1879, and there is a Georgian hudd, a sort of sentry box to protect the parson from the rain at a graveside.

In the 1870s the French poet, Paul Verlaine, came to teach in Friskney. He lived quietly, a changed character from the man who had recently come out of prison after shooting and wounding his close friend, the blazing young genius Rimbaud. Verlaine stayed at first in a little building by the school, where a photograph of him is displayed, and later opposite the church. After a while Verlaine moved to Boston, and then to Bournemouth before returning to France, to fame and some of his old habits.

Off one of the little fen roads a path leads to the Lincolnshire Trust nature reserve which holds Friskney Decoy Pond, partially restored. It was in use until about 1870. In the great days of wildfowling, Defoe says, decoy ducks were taught to fly as far as Holland and Germany, where they informed native ducks, 'in Language that they make one another understand', the benefits of coming to England. Most decoy ducks seem to have stayed on the pond, sometimes aided by swimming terriers which drove the wild birds along narrow channels or pipes into the nets. Decoy ducks were enticed to swim towards the nets by hemp seed scattered on the water. According to report, the wildfowl were so shy that the smell of a saucepan of burned milk would scare all the ducks away, though why a fowler should be boiling milk is not explained. He was apparently otherwise engaged, for a trick of his was to burn turf and hold a smouldering piece of it in front of his mouth so that the ducks couldn't smell him. Perhaps the milk was to settle his stomach, if his breath was so rank. Or he may have eaten too many cranberries, of which there were acres around Friskney.

While the Fens were still 'woosie', in Michael Drayton's phrase,

Lincolnshire was known as the aviary of England. Camden is one of the writers who gave long lists of birds to be found, not only 'the common ones which are in great esteem in other places . . . but such as have no Latin names, the delicacies of the tables and the food for heroes, fit for the palates of the great'. In 1515 lapwings, knots and dotterels fetched 1d each; seagulls, plovers, woodcocks and redshanks 1½d; pigeons, terns and snipes 3 for 1d; stints 6 for 1d; ruffs, reeves (the female) and partridges 2d each; bitterns and curlews 1½d each. In 1790 a ruff and a reeve sold for five shillings the couple, but by then their numbers, in Lord Torrington's words, had been 'thinned by voluptuousness and agriculture'.

By Friskney it is not altogether clear whether we are in the Fens or the Marsh. More or less officially, the Fens end at Wainfleet, on the Steeping River, which many pages back we observed flowing into the sea at Gibraltar Point. I wish we were there again, setting out on this tour of Lincolnshire.

Index